W9-BNO-628

User's Guide to the AAMFT Code of Ethics

Published by the American Association
for Marriage and Family Therapy
Alexandria, VA

The American Association for Marriage and Family Therapy

promotes and advances the common professional

interests of Marriage and Family Therapists.

This document is published by:

The American Association for Marriage and Family Therapy

112 South Alfred Street

Alexandria, VA 22314-3061

703-838-9808

© 2006 American Association for Marriage and Family Therapy
All rights reserved. Printed in the United States of America. No part of this
publication may be reproduced, stored in a retrieval system, or transmitted, in
any form or by any means, electronic, mechanical, photocopying, recording,
or otherwise, without the prior written permission of the publisher.

Middle of the night, December 4, 1989. No one aboard the *Mesquite* had noticed their drift after picking up a buoy and securing it on deck. Now the *Mesquite* was hard aground in the shoals just off Keweenaw Point, with her 12-foot draft sitting in 11 feet of dark, icy water off an inhospitable wilderness shore with no lights in sight. The pounding waves raised and dropped the ship on the rocks steadily, slowly puncturing the hull in several places. By 6:30 A.M., the engine room was flooded and the command to abandon ship was given. The crew took lifeboats to the nearby ocean-going ship, a visiting "saltie" from India, the *Mangal Desai*, that had responded to their distress transmissions. Five days later, another storm tore off *Mesquite's* rudder, toppled a mast, and put more holes into her torn steel bottom. Salvage now seemed beyond hope, although 19,000 gallons of diesel fuel were successfully removed. The replacement cost of such a vessel was $44,000,000, but even so, the Coast Guard abandoned the *Mesquite* two weeks later. Lake Superior added one more shipwreck to her long list.

Within days, two Michigan groups vied for the *Mesquite's* sinking rights. The Alger Underwater Preserve at Munising, Michigan, and the (then-) proposed Keweenaw Underwater Preserve where the *Mesquite* already lay, both wanted the rights to the battered ship for the creation of a new scuba dive site. Both indicated that the scuba diving community would treat this shipwreck with respect. The bid to remove the *Mesquite* as scrap was a lofty $4,000,000. In the end, the *Mesquite* was stripped of its superstructure (which was later dumped in pieces next to *Mesquite's* hull), lifted off the reef by the cranes of an enormous barge, and scuttled on July 15, 1990, in 115' of water just off Keystone Bay a mile and a half from where she had grounded. The ship sits upright and is still considerably intact, even without the superstructure in place. Office equipment, clothing, and galley supplies are among the many items that were left on board.

Within months of the scuttling of the *Mesquite*, a minority of thoughtless, lawbreaking scuba divers, desperate for the "glory" of possessing a part of the *Mesquite* as a souvenir of their visit, or as a "token of accomplishment," began tearing the insides, the very heart, of this vessel apart. They did not care that they were kicking the teeth out of a World War II veteran. They stole plates, silverware, brass fittings, and fixtures, prompting law enforcement agencies to tighten surveillance of the site and investigate reports of certain sport divers' residences displaying this stolen property. These thefts prompted one disgusted Lake Superior writer to publicize the matter: "...Plundering of the wreck began immediately. Using pry bars, tire irons and hammers, the wreck is being reduced to empty and dark passages, devoid of any sign of its former life. The large majority of divers is dismayed, but the looting continues. In just a few weeks, this small segment of divers has set wreck preservation back a generation. Their conduct lends support to new laws that will soon threaten their sport. Because of their actions, the time is coming when all wrecks will be off-limits...." These ominous words were penned by a longtime scuba diver who remembered the destructive free-for-all that divers had with shipwrecks in the 1960's. He does not wish to return to those irresponsible days.

ABOVE: *All embarrassing reminders that this accident happened to a Coast Guard vessel were removed before the* MESQUITE *was scuttled in deep water in the summer of 1990. This official Coast Guard insignia on the bow was somehow overlooked.* BELOW: *Below deck on the* MESQUITE *after the scuttling, it looked as though business was meant to go on as usual. Most items, including these filing cabinets still full of documents, were left behind.* PHOTOS BY PETER TOMASINO.

Moore, Smith   (#15 on the map on p. 355)

VESSEL NAME:	SMITH MOORE
RIG:	wooden steamer
DIMENSIONS:	223' 4" x 35' x 18' 2"
LAUNCHED:	Thursday, July 29, 1880; Cleveland, Ohio
DATE LOST:	Saturday, July 13, 1889
CAUSE OF LOSS:	collision with the JAMES PICKANDS
CARGO:	iron ore
LIVES LOST:	none (from 15 crew + family passengers)
GENERAL LOCATION:	East Channel of Munising Bay, Michigan
DEPTH:	91' - 105'
ACCESS:	boat
DIVING SKILL LEVEL:	advanced
DIVING HAZARDS:	depth, hypothermia, darkness, boating traffic
CO-ORDINATES:	Lat/Lon: 46.27.33 / 86.37.06
	Loran: 31642.2 / 47442.1

In the summer of 1889, three Great Lakes ships which all eventually ended up on the bottom of Lake Superior were involved in a tense drama off Munising, Michigan. The 223' wooden steamer, *Smith Moore*, had departed Munising loaded with 1,743 tons of iron ore, at 2:00 A.M., July 13, 1889, downbound towards Cleveland. Two hours later, in dense fog, she collided with the 232' wooden steamer, *James Pickands*, about ten miles off Grand Island. Visibility being limited to about 300', both ships were blowing foghorn warnings. Captain Clinton Ennis on the *Pickands* had heard the *Moore's* foghorn, but, due to the science of sound traveling in fog, could not tell from which direction it was coming. He found out when the *Moore's* massive bow appeared ghost-like out of the shroud of night-time fog heading towards his ship slightly to port. Both ships attempted to steer clear of each other, but still struck a glancing blow. Since the *Pickands* was light (traveling with no cargo), she simply bounced off the other hull, resulting in only cosmetic damage to the *Pickands*. Thinking that the same thing had happened to the other ship, and hearing no distress sounds coming from the *Moore* which had drifted off somewhere into the foggy night, Captain Ennis and the *James Pickands* proceeded towards Marquette.

But the *Smith Moore* was in serious trouble. Her bow had been pierced and broken in the collision, and she was taking on water fast. She sounded distress signals which the *Pickands* apparently did not hear. Preparations were made to lower the lifeboats from the *Smith Moore*, and the command was given to head for nearby Grand Island at full steam.

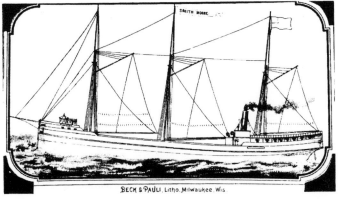

The wooden steamer, SMITH MOORE *(1880-1889).* AUTHOR'S COLLECTION.

Meanwhile, the 201' wooden steamer, *M.M. Drake* eventually came within earshot of the *Smith Moore's* distress signals and raced to the scene. A line was attached to the mortally wounded *Moore*, most of her people boarded the *Drake,* and the slowly sinking ship was taken in tow back towards Munising. They almost made it. At about 10:00 A.M., the *Drake* was straining to reach the shallows of Munising harbor with her crippled and increasingly heavy tow, when the *Smith Moore* sank. The line was cut, the remaining crew were removed, and their ship disappeared in 105' of water off Sand Point, a short distance to the east of Munising harbor. Her stern cabin, pilot house, and other wooden debris broke to the surface, while her masts protruded from the water about 15'. Hardhat diver John Quinn found the hull in good shape, but the cargo pre-empted salvage.

Ironically, both the ship that sank the *Smith Moore* and the ship that tried to save her ended their careers on the bottom of Lake Superior. The *James Pickands*, offshore in blinding forest fire smoke on Sept. 27, 1894, stranded on Sawtooth Reef off the Keweenaw and became a total loss (see pp. 438-439). The *M.M. Drake* sank off Whitefish Point on Oct. 2, 1901, in a collision incurred while attempting to re-attach to her tow. No lives were lost in either loss. Capt. Smith Moore, co-owner of his namesake, mastered the *Pickands* at one time.

It was during July, 1966, 77 years after the *Smith Moore* sank, that two teams of Michigan scuba divers, working in competition, stripped most of the artifacts from the shipwreck in their quest for the mythical 350 barrels of whiskey and 150 barrels of silver ore that were supposedly on board. They brought up only blocks, crocks, steam gauges, ventilator covers, brass hardware, and galley equipment, including a big kettle that they bragged was probably worth about $100 as an antique. A newspaper photo showed three of these divers with many of their artifact recoveries. Times change.

The *Smith Moore*, upright with her engine cylinders, boiler, and many more items, is a popular site in Michigan's Alger Underwater Preserve.

A steam winch on the SMITH MOORE'S *deck interests a visiting diver. Even the dynamite damage done by divers who removed her anchors in the late 1960's does not detract too much from what is left. Yet it could be better.* PHOTO BY CRIS KOHL.

In 1986-87, nearby Sand Point shifted considerably and, true to its name, moved sand onto the SMITH MOORE *site. Of the steam engine, only the tops of the cylinders remain uncovered, framed here by the main steam pipe. Other items remaining at this buoyed site include capstans, mooring bitts, and pumps.* PHOTO BY CRIS KOHL.

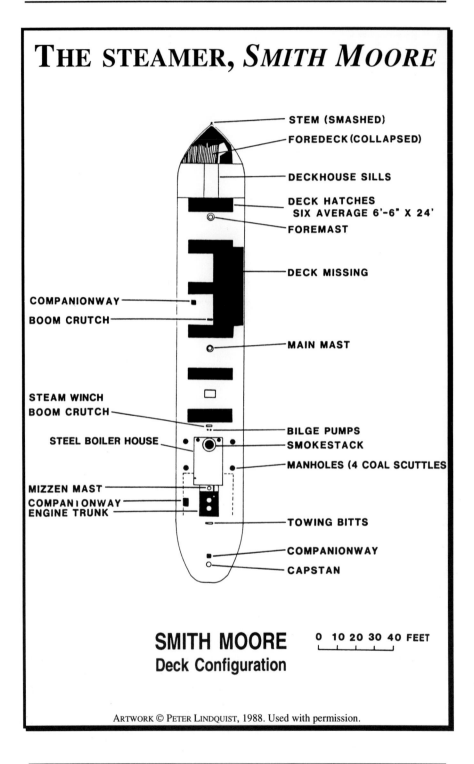

THE STEAMER, *SMITH MOORE*

SMITH MOORE
Deck Configuration

0 10 20 30 40 FEET

ARTWORK © PETER LINDQUIST, 1988. Used with permission.

Myron

(#16 on the map on p. 355)

VESSEL NAME:	MYRON; launched as MARK HOPKINS
RIG:	wooden steamer
DIMENSIONS:	186' x 32' 6" x 13'
LAUNCHED:	1888; Grand Haven, Michigan
DATE LOST:	Saturday, November 22, 1919
CAUSE OF LOSS:	foundered in a storm
CARGO:	lumber
LIVES LOST:	17 (from 18 on board)
GENERAL LOCATION:	3 miles w-n-w of Whitefish Point, Michigan
DEPTH:	42' - 50'
ACCESS:	boat
DIVING SKILL LEVEL:	novice-intermediate
DIVING HAZARDS:	hypothermia, disorientation, silting
CO-ORDINATES:	Lat/Lon: 46.48.463 / 85.01.646
	Loran: 31142.9 / 47566.5

The 186' steamer, *Myron,* and her consort, the 202' schooner-barge, *Miztec,* were partners who had weathered many Lake Superior gales together while hauling huge loads of lumber. Unfortunately, at the age of 31, the *Myron's* time was running out.

The *Myron* could load a respectable 700,000 board feet of lumber (about 950 gross tons). In the late 1890's, she often towed the equally-loaded schooner-barges, the *Edward Kelly* and the *Racine,* but in the early 1900's, the *Miztec* became the *Myron's* partner, and the two of them became very familiar sights hauling huge cargoes of lumber around the Great Lakes. The *Miztec* was one of the largest capacity towbarges in operation at that time, capable of carrying 1,050,000 board feet of lumber.

The *Myron* and *Miztec* were docked at Munising, Michigan, on the morning of Saturday, November 22, 1919, being loaded high with lumber under the watchful eye of the *Myron's* master, Captain Walter R. Neal. He kept his other eye with apprehension upon the increasingly restless conditions on Lake Superior. It was getting late in the shipping season, and he was aware of November pitfalls in weather. He was also aware of his responsibilities for two ships, almost two million board feet of lumber cargo, and, most importantly, the lives of 25 men, 18 on the *Myron,* and seven on the *Miztec.*

Captain Neal decided to make the run towards Sault Ste. Marie. Unfortunately, the *Myron* and the *Miztec* ran headlong into a violent storm, with northwest winds blowing 60 miles an hour. By 2:00 P.M., with the *Myron* leaking so badly that the pumps had difficulty keeping the below-deck water level down, Neal, an excellent navigator, ran the *Myron* close by the *Miztec* and yelled to the barge captain that he was going to cut the towline. Tied together in these dangerous winds and rolling waves, the two ships ran the risk of colliding. Besides, towbarges were equipped to be able to fend for themselves in an emergency. Together, the *Myron* was incapable of making any progress.

This was indeed an emergency. Ice had formed on the *Myron*, weighing her down and forcing her to float lower than usual in the tumultuous water. This in turn retarded her forward progress, even with the steam engine at full power. The problem of water washing over the gunwales, penetrating the hull, and collecting in the bilge and beyond was very real. Captain Neal only hoped that now, with the *Myron's* engine responsible for propelling only one ship, they would reach the safety of Whitefish Bay's calmer waters a few miles ahead of them.

Also trying to reach Whitefish Bay, but not in as desperate a situation as the *Myron,* was the 420' steel steamer, *Adriatic.* At 3:00 P.M., both vessels were struggling off Crisp Point, but the *Myron* was the only one sending distress signals. The crew could not control the water rising in her hold. At 4:20 P.M., with the darkness of the late autumn and the storm fully upon her, the *Myron* was only three miles from Whitefish Point, and a mile-and-a-half off shore. But she stopped suddenly. The rising water below deck had reached the boiler fire and extinguished it. Now the *Myron* was really in trouble!

Captain Neal ordered the 17 men in his crew into the two lifeboats, which they filled and launched in record time. However, Neal was from the old school of thought, believing that the captain should stay with his vessel and, if need be, go down with the ship. He declined to board a lifeboat.

The *Myron* sank within five minutes of the boiler fire dying and, as she did, an immense wave tore the wooden pilothouse off the steamer. Captain Neal clung to the roof of the pilothouse as it disappeared out into the open lake.

The *Adriatic,* joined by another steel steamer, *H.P. McIntosh,* and a Coast Guard rescue vessel, dodged the floating lumber cargo while attempting to reach the *Myron's* lifeboats. But darkness had fallen, and trying to maneuver their ships close to the storm-tossed lifeboats in a sea laced with bobbing timber was impossible. At one point, the *McIntosh* was close enough to toss a line, but the crew in the lifeboat could not hold on to it. The wind and the waves again parted them, and the lifeboats disappeared into the night.

At noon the next day, with the storm still raging, Captain W.C. Jordon of the steamer, *W.C. Franz,* sighted the floating pilothouse with the unconscious, nearly dead body of Captain Neal on top of it near Parisienne Island

ABOVE: *The wooden steamer,* MYRON, *was built at Grand Haven, Michigan, in 1888.* BELOW: *After the violent storm that sank the* MYRON *on November 22, 1919, with the loss of 17 of the 18 people on board, debris, including this large stern section of the ship, washed ashore on the Canadian side.* GREAT LAKES MARINE COLLECTION OF THE MILWAUKEE PUBLIC LIBRARY/WISCONSIN MARINE HISTORICAL SOCIETY.

on the Canadian side of Whitefish Bay. In the preceding 20 hours, this raft had been swept 20 miles from the place where the *Myron* sank! Captain Jordon thought the man on the pilothouse was dead, but sent a lifeboat to investigate when he noticed some movement in one of his hands. Captain Neal was taken to Port Arthur, Ontario on board the *Franz*. There, he denounced the crew of the *McIntosh*, claiming that they had refused to pick him up, replying to his appeal for help with a promise to send a tug to get him!

STEAMER MYRON GOES DOWN IN SUPERIOR GALE

Hope Entertained That Some Members of Crew of Eighteen May Have Survived Freezing Blizzard.

Headlines about the loss of the MYRON, TOLEDO BLADE, *November 24, 1919.*

The rescue of Captain Neal inspired hope that others from the *Myron* would be found alive. Coast Guard submarine chaser number 438, unsuccessful at finding work in her usual line of employment since World War I had ended a year earlier, left Sault Ste. Marie, Michigan, with a double crew in quest of more *Myron* survivors. The sub chaser failed at that job. All 17 men in the two *Myron* lifeboats were lost to Lake Superior. Three days after the sinking, the Kingston, Ontario, newspaper proclaimed, "...Little hope is held out, however, that *[Myron]* bodies would wash ashore, unless lashed to wreckage, as the cold lake waters prevent forming of gases, and, it is claimed bodies seldom rise to the surface. It is traditional that 'Lake Superior seldom gives up its dead.'"

The *Myron's* faithful towbarge, the *Miztec*, survived the storm and was towed into Whitefish Bay by the freighter, *Argus*.

One lifeboat of *Myron* sailors, all frozen to death, was found by a tug in Whitefish Bay. In the spring of 1920, eight bodies were found in the melting, shoreline ice near Salt Point. They were all chopped out of the ice and buried, in box coffins made at the nearby Evans mill, in an old Indian cemetery at Mission Hill overlooking Iroquois Point. A recently-restored wooden fence encloses these sailors' graves among the pines. The original sign marking the site stated simply, "Sailors of the Steamer, *Myron*." Today, a second sign tells their story.

ABOVE: *Captain Walter Roger Neal, who decided to stay with his sinking ship, ended up as its sole survivor.* GREAT LAKES MARINE COLLECTION OF THE MILWAUKEE PUBLIC LIBRARY/WISCONSIN MARINE HISTORICAL SOCIETY. BELOW: *Eight bodies from the steamer,* MYRON, *were chopped out of shoreline ice the following spring, and were interred on Mission Hill Cemetery overlooking Iroquois Point.* PHOTO BY CRIS KOHL.

Built by John Callister for Mark Hopkins of St. Clair, Michigan, and launched as the *Mark Hopkins* in 1888 at Grand Haven, Michigan, the 676-gross-ton wooden steamer was renamed *Myron* in 1902, after Mr. Myron Baker (1896-1955), the sole son of the vessel's 1902 owner, Captain Harris W. Baker. The *Myron,* official number 91993, measured 186' in length, 32' 6" in beam, and 13' in draft. She was rebuilt at Duluth in the spring of 1904. Her fore & aft compound engine, built by S.F. Hodge & Company of Detroit in 1888, and her Buffalo-built Scotch boiler (constructed in 1890 and installed some time between 1909 and 1914; her first boiler was a fire box type from 1888 built by the Johnston Brothers of Ferrysburg, Michigan) produced 700 horsepower, ample strength for the fully loaded steamer and her tow to still slice through northern waters. But she failed to outrun that fateful 1919 storm on Lake Superior.

As the *Mark Hopkins,* the ship had one serious accident on September 23, 1895, when it sank in a collision with the 235' steamer, *Vanderbilt,* in the St. Mary's River. The *Hopkins* was raised, repaired and returned to service.

Today, the *Myron's* remains, located by scuba divers in 1972, lie in relatively shallow water three miles west-northwest from Whitefish Point. The boiler and engine, with brass valves and fittings, sit off to the port side a bit and are definitely worth studying. Check out the ship's tools laid out next to the engine. The stern also yields a metal capstan. Most of the mid-section of the hull has broken up because ice and waves penetrate this shallow depth (55'), but the enormous, four-bladed, upright propeller is a necessary stop. Following the mostly buried outline of the keel, visiting scuba divers will recognize a spare propeller blade sitting on the deck. A large windlass lies just off the bow, and metal tie-downs, used in securing lumber to the deck, can also be seen in the bow area. The *Myron's* wooden bow, for now, remains upright and impressive, decoratively draped with the ship's anchor chains which disappear into the sandy bottom (see the photo on the front cover of this book).

Early divers recovered an anchor from the *Myron* and donated it to the Valley Camp Marine Museum at Sault Ste. Marie, Michigan.

There is one more interesting detail to tell in the tragic story of the steamer, *Myron*. The towbarge *Miztec,* orphaned after the *Myron's* loss, was adopted by the steamer, *Zillah*. During a heavy spring storm on May 13, 1921, only 18 months after her forced separation from the *Myron* and nearing the spot where her old steamer-consort lay, the *Miztec,* seemingly with a mind of her own, mysteriously broke loose from the *Zillah,* filled with water in the blizzard-like weather conditions, and sank with the loss of all seven men on board. Both ships, the *Myron* and the *Miztec,* were exactly 31 years old when they sank in storms, both shipwrecks rest in exactly 45' to 55' of water, and, as if by choice, the *Miztec* lies close to her beloved, old partner, the *Myron,* , together forever.

Diver Joan Forsberg glides past the MYRON'S *bow anchor chains, which form an artistic drape dipping into Lake Superior's undulating sands.* PHOTO BY CRIS KOHL.

ABOVE: *The* MYRON'S *midship section is totally collapsed, with the keel being the only visible guide between bow and stern. Divers Dr. Gary Elliott and Joan Forsberg follow it across the wet desert sands at 50'.* BELOW: *The* MYRON'S *steam engine and the remains of the rest of her propulsion system lie broken and clustered at the stern. The immense boiler is off to the port side of the stern.* PHOTOS BY CRIS KOHL.

Panther

(#17 on the map on p. 355)

VESSEL NAME:	PANTHER
RIG:	wooden steamer
DIMENSIONS:	247' 6" x 35' 8" x 22' 2"
LAUNCHED:	1890; West Bay City, Michigan
DATE LOST:	Monday, June 26, 1916
CAUSE OF LOSS:	collision with steamer, JAMES J. HILL
CARGO:	wheat
LIVES LOST:	none
GENERAL LOCATION:	off Parisienne Island, Whitefish Bay
DEPTH:	88' - 110'
ACCESS:	boat
DIVING SKILL LEVEL:	advanced
DIVING HAZARDS:	depth, silting, hypothermia
CO-ORDINATES:	Lat/Lon: 46.38.40 / 84.48.29
	Loran: 31105.8 / 47685.9

The first time I spent quality time scuba diving in Lake Superior in the 1980's, I was astounded at the way fogbanks rolled in and out continuously all day and all night long. Having spent most of my life, and much of my diving, in the southern half of the Great Lakes, this was an unfamiliar phenomenon.

Apparently, many sailors on the inland seas years ago felt the same way. A fair number of "greenhorn" crews, not experienced with the way Lake Superior works, and in charge of ships built down in the lower half, succumbed to the raw weather in this unrefined region.

The wooden steamer, *Panther,* was built "down south" by James Davidson at West Bay City, Michigan, in 1890 (official #150497). The massive, 1,634-gross-ton ship measured 247' 6" in length, with a beam of 35' 8" and a draft of 22' 2". Her fore & aft compound engine and huge Scotch boiler delivered 600 horsepower, enough to cruise her along at a fair speed while fully loaded, usually with grain. Rebuilt at Chicago in 1901, the *Panther* had one dangerous experience when she was sunk near Garden Island in Lake Michigan on November 21, 1910. Raised and repaired, the ship sailed the Great Lakes for a total of 26 years before falling permanent prey to Lake Superior's fog.

On May 19, 1916, the American Steamship Company of Duluth sold the *Panther* to the Massey Steamship Company of Fort William, Ontario. The transaction was completed just in time. Five weeks later, the ship sank.

The wooden steamer, PANTHER, *served the Great Lakes from 1890 until 1916, when a collision with the much larger steel ship,* JAMES J. HILL, *sent her to the bottom of Whitefish Bay in Lake Superior.* GREAT LAKES MARINE COLLECTION OF THE MILWAUKEE PUBLIC LIBRARY/WISCONSIN MARINE HISTORICAL SOCIETY.

Captain Peter Shaw watched closely as his charge, the *Panther,* sliced through the dark waters of Whitefish Bay. He estimated that his ship, loaded with 65,000 bushels of wheat downbound from Fort William, Ontario, was just off Parisienne Island, approaching the Soo. The time was 10:30 P.M. on Mon., June 26, 1916. He felt uncomfortable about the ship cutting through the dense fog so easily. With extremely limited visibility, this was very dangerous sailing.

Steaming equally blindly through the same fog was the upbound steamer, *James J. Hill,* which had just emerged from the Soo locks and was traveling light to pick up a shipment of iron ore. With a length of 478', the *Hill* was almost twice the length of the *Panther.* With a hull of steel rather than wood, the *Hill* was a dangerous torpedo speeding through the night and the fog.

Without much warning, the *Hill* appeared out of the thick fog, and Captain Shaw watched in horror as the huge, steel bow pierced his old ship's wooden hull. It was an eternity before the *Hill* came to a stop. By that time, the *Panther* was almost bisected. Captain Shaw knew that his ship would sink.

Captain George Randall on the *James J. Hill* also knew that the un-identified wooden steamer they had just struck was doomed. He kept his presence of mind while keeping the *Hill's* bow firmly embedded in the *Panther's* midship starboard side. This allowed the *Panther's* crew enough time to jump aboard the *Hill.* When the *Hill* backed away, the fatally injured *Panther* rapidly filled with water from the gaping hole in her side, listed heavily to the port side, then turned over and sank in about 100' of water. Twenty minutes expired between the collision and the sinking. The aging *Panther*, valued at $15,000, and her $65,000 cargo of new wheat, were both uninsured. The 5,000-gross-ton *Hill*, only slightly damaged, returned to Sault Ste. Marie with the orphaned crew, and continued on her upbound journey to Duluth the next day. The *James J. Hill's* namesake, Mr. James Jerome Hill, president of the Great Northern Railway System, had died on May 29, 1916, just four weeks before the ship named after him rammed into the *Panther*. The *Hill*, built at Lorain, Ohio, in 1900, served the Great Lakes until the ship was sunk as a breakwater at Cleveland in 1961.

The wreck of the *Panther* sits in 88' to 110' of water, upright and reasonably intact, considering the collision and her long drop to the rocky lake bottom. The decks have collapsed and the sides of the hull have sprung outward. A number of interesting items to be viewed on deck include tools, dishes, portholes, and burbots. The stern area is of the greatest interest, since it is more intact than the bow. It contains the rudder and rudder post, which was pushed up through the decking and stands "at attention" on the lake bottom. The engine, smokestack, boiler, large winch, and stove are attention grabbers, while it is easy to scoop up a handful of the wheat that sits loaded to the top of the hatch openings and watch the kernels flow between your fingers back into the hold. This site, part of the Whitefish Point Underwater Preserve, is usually buoyed.

The stern area of the steamer, PANTHER, *is interesting due to sights such as the rudder, engine, and boiler, as well as this steam-powered winch.*   PHOTO BY CRIS KOHL.

Pickands, James

(#18 on the map on p. 355)

VESSEL NAME:	JAMES PICKANDS
RIG:	wooden steamer
DIMENSIONS:	232' 6" x 40' x 19' 2"
LAUNCHED:	1886; Cleveland, Ohio
DATE LOST:	Saturday, September 22, 1894
CAUSE OF LOSS:	stranded
CARGO:	iron ore
LIVES LOST:	none (from 15 on board)
GENERAL LOCATION:	Eagle River Reef, Keweenaw Peninsula
DEPTH:	10' - 30'
ACCESS:	boat
DIVING SKILL LEVEL:	novice
DIVING HAZARDS:	minimal; poor visibility sometimes
CO-ORDINATES:	Lat/Lon: 47.25.46 / 88.18.02
	Loran: 31825.1 / 46553.2

The 232' 6" wooden steamer, *James Pickands*, had close calls and made a few headlines in her brief career before she finally sank in 1894. The *Pickands* was accidentally instrumental in the sinking of the steamer, *Smith Moore*, at Munising on July 13, 1889 (see pp. 422-425). That collision left the *James Pickands* with a few scrapes on her bow. The *Pickands*, according to the Lifesaving Report of 1894, stranded in foggy weather at Two Heart River on Lake Superior on July 5, 1893. After jettisoning 75 tons of her iron ore cargo, she was successfully pulled off by the passing steamer, *Joliet*. The Lifesaving crews from Two Heart River and Crisps Station nearby had helped jettison the cargo, receiving praise from Captain Beach. A year later, it would take a lot more than help in throwing the cargo overboard to save the *James Pickands*.

Serious forest fires in northern Minnesota and Wisconsin in the late summer of 1894 destroyed more than just wilderness forests and its fauna. Smoke clouds lay low over the lakes, producing at first a blue haze and later a darker, more serious visual impediment. It was in these conditions that the steamer, *James Pickands*, bound from Duluth to south Chicago with a small load of iron ore, wandered off course and struck the rocks on Sawtooth Reef near Eagle River on the Keweenaw Peninsula on September 22, 1894.

Captain Beach, as a wise precaution, removed himself and his crew to the nearby shore in a lifeboat, and wired the news of the accident to the ship's owners in Cleveland. The newspaper reports offer a detailed account of the loss:

"The big steamer, *James Pickands*, with ore from the head of Lake Superior to Cleveland, is on Eagle River reef, in Lake Superior and will be, with her cargo, a total loss. Advices of the wreck reached the owners here this morning in a dispatch from Captain C.H. Beach. The dispatch stated that the decks were burst open amidships, and that the hold was full of water. The bottom was also caved in, and the steamer lies on her port sides on her beams ends, on a rocky bottom. Eagle River reef, the place where stranding took place, is just to the westward of Keweenaw Point. here is a long list of wrecked boats recorded against this spot, and few boats striking here are released. The *Pickands* had 1,500 tons of iron ore for Ogleby, Norton & Co., of this place. The boat is owned by Captain John W. Moore, Robert R. Rhodes, Captain Al Manning, and Pickands, Mather & Co., of Cleveland. All have their interests well covered [author's note: this meant that they had each insured their share of the ship].... She is valued at $85,000. Captain Beach, her master, is well known on the lakes and formerly commanded one of the whaleback steamers.... The owners of the *Pickands* this afternoon abandoned the wreck to the underwriters. Captain Beach telegraphed that a large rock has been forced through the bottom amidships. The deck amidships has been raised eight feet.... The wrecking tug *Favorite* will go to the *Pickands* as a forlorn hope, it being agreed that the wrecking bill will be 'satisfactory' to the underwriters if the steamer is not saved...."

Two days later, the news was reported that a heavy sea prevailed, much of the *Pickands'* loose machinery was washed away, and the boat had nearly gone to pieces. Captain Beach and a representative of the underwriters remained near the wreck scene for a few more days. On Oct. 2, 1894, the Pickands' machinery and boilers were sold to Joseph Croze of nearby Houghton, Michigan, from the insurance company for $1,000. The newspaper printed a curt "Nothing remains of the boat," and Mr. Croze never did remove the large pieces of machinery which he had purchased. Perhaps the underwriters' representative at the scene of the shipwreck had quite the smooth tongue and sold land in Florida on the side.

The ship was valued at $85,000 at the time of loss, with her small cargo worth a paltry $3,200. Built in 1886 at Cleveland, Ohio, by Thomas Quayle & Son, this 1,545-gross-ton wooden steamer had three masts and twin smokestacks and carried coarse freight throughout her short, eight-year life.

Today, the broken and scattered wreckage of the *James Pickands* sits high on Sawtooth Reef, mingled with the remains of two other ships destroyed at this site, namely the *Colorado,* a 252' wooden steamer which stranded and broke up here on Sept. 19, 1898, another victim of forest fire smoke, and the 65' tug, *Fern,* which wrecked here on June 29, 1901, losing its entire crew of five who were attempting to salvage scrap metal from the *Colorado.* This combined shipwrecks site, in 10' to 30' of water, has quite a violent history crammed into a small area. The *Pickands'* boilers and rudder are the main attractions.

Rappahannock   (#19 on the map on p. 355)

VESSEL NAME:	RAPPAHANNOCK
RIG:	wooden steamer
DIMENSIONS:	308' 1" x 42' 5" x 21' 2"
LAUNCHED:	Thursday, June 6, 1895; West Bay City, MI
DATE LOST:	Tuesday, July 25, 1911
CAUSE OF LOSS:	stranded
CARGO:	coal
LIVES LOST:	none (from 18 on board)
GENERAL LOCATION:	Jackfish Bay, Ontario (north shore)
DEPTH:	35' - 85'
ACCESS:	boat; shore dive from Jackfish Bay
DIVING SKILL LEVEL:	intermediate-advanced
DIVING HAZARDS:	depth, penetration, darkness, current
CO-ORDINATES:	Lat/Lon:
	Loran:

The large wooden steamer, *Rappahannock*, was already leaking badly on the open waters of Lake Superior when a mid-summer storm pounded the ship with 70 mile-an-hour winds. Captain W.A. Ratley, of Algonac, MI, knew that it was time to retreat. His commendable crew, sweating from hours of non-stop pumping to keep them afloat, could not be expected to show such strength much longer. The only safe retreat was Jackfish Bay, on the north shore in Canada.

The ship and her tow, the 360' barge *Montezuma*, were both loaded with coal from Ashtabula, Ohio, heading towards Duluth. They stayed close to the lake's north shore to avoid a possible collision with ships in the usual traffic route. At 4:00 A.M., Monday, July 24, 1911, the *Rappahannock's* mate reported that the boat was taking on water. The wind, already strong, worsened. The towline to the barge broke at 5:30 A.M. and the ships were separated (the tow was later picked up by another steamer). By 11:00 A.M., the *Rappahannock*, with six feet of water in her hold, was in serious trouble. The crew ran the ship towards Jackfish Bay, arriving after dark at 10:30 P.M. At that point, the steering gave out, but they managed to run her aground at 11:00 P.M. But instead of being able to stay put and relax, the tired crew soon realized that the stern, hanging over deep water, was sinking. They abandoned ship in lifeboats at 12:40 A.M., and the ship sank 25 minutes later. They camped that night on the shore.

The 308' 1" RAPPAHANNOCK, one of the last wooden steamers to be built, was constructed by James Davidson for James Davidson at West Bay City, Michigan, in 1895, official #111083, 2,380 gross tons. AUTHOR'S COLLECTION.

The RAPPAHANNOCK offers visiting scuba divers views of carved wooden supports holding up the covered walkway, as well as open doorways rich in the kind of textured wood that can be found only on Great Lakes shipwrecks. PHOTO BY JOYCE HAYWARD.

The water in Jackfish Bay turns from green to black with depth and conditions. This photo was taken in 1989 the day after the stolen ship's wheel was returned to the RAPPAHANNOCK *site and chained to a portion of the shallow bow. Unfortunately, the wheel disappeared again in 1995.* PHOTO BY CRIS KOHL.

The *Rappahannock*, found by Ryan LeBlanc in 1979, is in excellent shape. The hull is intact, with a capstan on deck. Several intact glass windows can be peeped into by the diver as s/he swims along the covered walkway, held up by carved, wooden supports. Below, there is a carpenter's bench, a stove with a pan on it, and much machinery, including an 1895 triple expansion steam engine built in Detroit. Recent rains may reduce visibility and light.

The wreck of the *Rappahannock* rests upright and mostly intact along a slope on the drop-off to deep water at the end of the eastern arm of Jackfish Bay, to the northeast of Observation Point. The wreck, sometimes marked with a buoy, sits under the high-voltage power line (the higher of the two) that runs across this arm of the bay. One way of getting to the site, if you have a small boat no longer than about 12' or beamier than about 4', is from Jackfish Lake heading towards Lake Superior, and entering an extremely narrow waterway tunnel under the Jackfish Bay railway culvert into Jackfish Bay. You may have to get out and pull or push the boat through. Again, anything bigger than an inflatable boat won't fit. Lift your outboard motor when traveling through this tunnel. From there, either take the boat directly to above the site, or leave the boat along the shoreline near the tunnel exit and swim out to the marker. You can also descend and follow the drop-off slope at a depth of 35' to 40', which would take you to the bow. Whichever way you reach this site, it will not be as difficult as it was for the *Rappahannock's* crew in their struggle to stay alive.

Sagamore

(#20 on the map on p. 355)

VESSEL NAME:	SAGAMORE
RIG:	whaleback steamer-barge
DIMENSIONS:	308' x 38' x 24'
LAUNCHED:	Saturday, July 23, 1892; Superior, WI
DATE LOST:	Monday, July 29, 1901
CAUSE OF LOSS:	collision with the NORTHERN QUEEN
CARGO:	iron ore
LIVES LOST:	3 (from 8 on board)
GENERAL LOCATION:	entrance to St. Mary's River, Whitefish Bay
DEPTH:	42' - 63'
ACCESS:	boat
DIVING SKILL LEVEL:	intermediate-advanced
DIVING HAZARDS:	boating traffic, depth, silting
CO-ORDINATES:	Lat/Lon: 46.31.089 / 84.37.927
	Loran: 31072.9 / 47771.8

The *Sagamore* is probably the best example of a whaleback steamer that can be found anywhere under the surface of the Great Lakes to date. Other shipwrecked whalebacks exist in the Great Lakes, like the *James B. Colgate* which lies upside-down in the middle of Lake Erie, and the fragmented pieces of the *Henry Cort* that lie scattered outside Muskegon harbor on Lake Michigan. The only remaining whaleback ship above water is the *Meteor*, now a museum ship on land at Superior, Wisconsin, and well worth a visit.

Whalebacks were the brainchild of a man named Alexander McDougall from Duluth. In the late 1880's, he designed a rounded, steel ship which resembled a pig-nosed, semi-submarine, or a long, slender, steel whale, with the idea that heavy seas would just roll off the streamlined contours of his unique creation. Forty-three whalebacks were constructed before the design proved too impractical, too small, and too uneconomical for hauling freight.

Monday, July 29, 1901, was foggy on Lake Superior's Whitefish Bay. Two whalebacks, the *Pathfinder* and her tow, the *Sagamore,* both heavily laden with iron ore bound from Duluth to Lake Erie, neared the Sault canal. Approaching from the Soo with a general cargo intended for Duluth was the steel steamer, *Northern Queen.* All three ships steamed into a hazardous sea of fogbanks from which only two of them would emerge.

At 10:40 A.M., the *Northern Queen* suddenly realized that she was on a collision course with the whaleback steamer, *Pathfinder,* which had suddenly appeared out of the fog. The helmsman on the *Northern Queen* quickly changed course. Unfortunately, because of the fog, he failed to see that he was turning into the *Pathfinder's* towbarge, the whaleback, *Sagamore.*

The *Northern Queen* plowed into the *Sagamore's* hull on the starboard side, near the after turret, and broke some steel plates. The *Sagamore* filled with water rapidly and reportedly sank in 12 fathoms, or 72' of water. The whaleback's crew dashed quickly onto the deck of the *Northern Queen*, five of them surviving the sinking of their ship. Three, however, perished in the collision: Captain E. Joiner, who lived in Henderson, New York, Ira Ives, the *Sagamore's* cook from Sacketts Harbor, New York, and sailor Burley Smith from Woodville, New York.

The *Northern Queen* returned to Sault Ste. Marie with the survivors and to make temporary repairs to her badly damaged hull. She eventually went into drydock for permanent repairs. The *Sagamore*, a permanent loss, was valued at $90,000.

The whaleback, or "pig boat," SAGAMORE.   GREAT LAKES MARINE COLLECTION OF THE MILWAUKEE PUBLIC LIBRARY/WISCONSIN MARINE HISTORICAL SOCIETY.

The *Sagamore's* keel was laid on Tuesday, December 15, 1891, and she was launched on Saturday, July 23, 1892, at Superior, Wisconsin. Her builder was the American Steel Barge Company, which sold her to the Huron Barge Company, managed by Pickands, Mather & Co., of Ashtabula, Ohio, within a few months of her launch. This 1,601-gross-ton ship, which measured 308' in length, 38' in beam, and 24' in draft, once unloaded a record 3,200 tons of iron ore in eight hours at Ashtabula, Ohio, in 1893. Her official number was 57932.

The wreck of the *Sagamore* sits upright, mostly intact, in 42' to 63' of water. The wide open hatches provide easy access and comfortable ambient light to make cautious, limited penetrations. A ladder descends into the forward part of the hatch nearest the bow (as if scuba divers needed a ladder to move from the deck into the hold!). Prisms, aligned in rows, allow light to access the cargo holds. For the forward two-thirds of this shipwreck, divers can swim through the inside of the hull, from hatchway to hatchway, never losing sight of an escape hatch if a quick exit becomes necessary.

Triple tow rings mounted atop the blunt-nosed bow are impressive and photogenic. Another set of triple tow rings lies flat in the torn and collapsed metal at the stern, over 300' away.

The triple tow rings on top of the blunt snout of the whaleback, SAGAMORE, *being examined by Dr. Gary Elliott, offer a dramatic and photogenic view. Whalebacks were nicknamed "pig boats" because of the unflattering nose.*   PHOTO BY CRIS KOHL.

This is a long shipwreck, and, for most of it, the scuba diver will be swimming past rusting metal sheet after rusting metal sheet. Near the stern, the extensive collision damage just forward of the after turret can be studied. The steel hull is definitely torn, twisted, and broken at this point. Gone is the smooth, rounded, streamlined hull that seemed endless. Here is the reason that three men died in 1901.

The Sagamore's *after turret still stands upright, although the stern portion of the shipwreck suffers from a decided list. It is on the other side of this turret that the collision damage to the* Sagamore *can be seen.* Photo by Cris Kohl.

        Unfortunately, the *Sagamore* site is not buoyed, making her difficult to locate. If she is buoyed, she won't be for long because she sits in the middle of the busy freighter shipping channel to and from the nearby Soo locks. Those big fellas have a way of inadvertently taking out marker buoys on shipwrecks. Wisely contact the U.S. Coast Guard at the Soo (906-635-3273, or VHF 16) to let them know you will be anchored over this site. They have been known to warn and redirect shipping traffic.

        It sure beats sitting there in your small boat, watching an enormous steel freighter heading straight for you, and wondering whether your right to be anchored at this shipwreck site will be overshadowed by the basic concept of "gross tonnage prevails."

Selvick, Steven M.

(#21 on the map on p. 355)

VESSEL NAME:	STEVEN M. SELVICK, ex-LORAIN
RIG:	steel tug
DIMENSIONS:	68' 7" x 17' x 11'
LAUNCHED:	1915; Cleveland, Ohio
DATE LOST:	Saturday, June 1, 1996
CAUSE OF LOSS:	scuttled
CARGO:	none
LIVES LOST:	none
GENERAL LOCATION:	6 miles north of Munising, Michigan
DEPTH:	45' - 65'
ACCESS:	boat
DIVING SKILL LEVEL:	novice-intermediate
DIVING HAZARDS:	minimal: penetration, silting
CO-ORDINATES:	Lat/Lon: 46.29.53 / 86.35.87
	Loran: 31629.3 / 47427.0

The tug, *Steven M. Selvick,* is a recent addition to the Great Lakes roster of shipwrecks, even though purists will argue that it doesn't really qualify as a shipwreck. However, it is a ship, and it does have a history, and it is wrecked at the bottom of the lake no longer capable of doing the usual work that a ship does, so it qualifies as a shipwreck. In this modern era, with genuine shipwrecks fortunately so few and far between, it is entirely acceptable to give shipwrecks an occasional helping hand by purposely planting them.

This 68' 7", 74-gross-ton, steel tug, hull number 34 of the Great Lakes Towing Company of Cleveland, Ohio, was launched in 1915 and given the name *Lorain,* with official number 212968. A variety of owners used this tug over the next 81 years: the Great Lakes Towing Company of Cleveland (1915-1942), the Huffman Construction Company of Buffalo (1942-1946), the U.S. Government (1946-1948), Merritt-Chapman & Scott Corp. of New York City (1948-1966) who changed the *Lorain's* name to *Cabot* in 1949, Andros Marine Chartering Company of Dania, Florida (1966-1967), the Providence Towing Corp. of Miami, Florida (1967-1971), Alan M. Kennedy, Jr. (1971-1972), and the Selvick Marine Towing Corporation of Sturgeon Bay, Wisconsin, from 1972 on. This last owner changed the ship's name from *Cabot* to *Steven M. Selvick* in honor of the owner's son in 1974. This tugboat's colorful history included helping in the construction of the Mackinac Bridge in 1957 by hauling steel. On a more personal level, the tug, *Steven M. Selvick,* was the site of namesake Steven M. Selvick's unique wedding reception on June 19, 1982.

The tug, SELVICK, *when she was named the* LORAIN. GREAT LAKES MARINE COLLECTION OF THE MILWAUKEE PUBLIC LIBRARY/WISCONSIN MARINE HISTORICAL SOCIETY.

In 1994, the Alger Underwater Preserve Committee, under President Peter Lindquist (who, incidentally, on May 24, 1992, officiated at the underwater wedding of two Lansing, Michigan, scuba divers on the nearby wreck of the *Smith Moore* --- see pp. 422-424 for that shipwreck's story), acquired the *Selvick* as a donation from her last owners. The tug was towed from Sturgeon Bay to Munising in the spring of 1994. During that tow, the *Selvick,* which had been idle for years and could no longer operate under her own power, reportedly came to life when her pilothouse searchlight suddenly came on one evening off Whitefish Point --- even though the batteries on board had all been disconnected! It is not the purpose of this book to comment on the symptoms and effects of psychological pressures arising from long voyages at sea.

At Munising, volunteers scrubbed all the oil and dirt off every part of the tug, and removed items which blocked safe diver access to the inside. Then, on June 1, 1996, the *Steven M. Selvick* joined the other shipwrecks in the Alger Underwater Preserve when her seacocks were opened in the company of a flotilla of small vessels. She slowly settled in 65' of water, with her profile rising 20' off the bottom. Only minimal damage --- the rudder broke off --- occurred when the vessel hit the bottom. Every area of this tugboat can be explored: the pilot house, the engine room, crew quarters, galley, and messroom. Doors have been secured in an open position, and an opening was cut into her deck to allow easy access to the stern. Thus, a modern shipwreck was created, offering scuba divers another excellent reason for visiting this part of the fantastic Great Lakes.

GOING,...

GOING,...

GONE!!! *The tug,* STEVEN M. SELVICK, *was scuttled as a new scuba dive site in Michigan's Alger Underwater Preserve near Munising on June 1, 1996.* PHOTOS BY CAPTAIN PETER LINDQUIST.

Sevona

(#22 on the map on p. 355)

VESSEL NAME:	SEVONA (launched as EMILY P. WEED)
RIG:	steel steamer
DIMENSIONS:	372' 5" x 41' x 24' 6"
LAUNCHED:	Saturday, June 7, 1890; West Bay City, MI
DATE LOST:	Saturday, September 2, 1905
CAUSE OF LOSS:	stranded
CARGO:	iron ore
LIVES LOST:	7 (from 24 on board)
GENERAL LOCATION:	Sand I. Reef, Apostle Islands, Wisconsin
DEPTH:	16' - 20'
ACCESS:	boat
DIVING SKILL LEVEL:	novice-intermediate
DIVING HAZARDS:	poor visibility sometimes
CO-ORDINATES:	Lat/Lon:
	Loran: 32388.1 / 46032.9

Early on the morning of Saturday, September 2, 1905, the 372' steel steamer, *Sevona*, with 24 people on board, including four women, ran aground on Sand Island Shoal about one and a half miles northeast of the island. The pounding seas were churned by tempestuous gales and the persistent rains clouded visions on board the ship. The weight of 6,000 tons of iron ore bore heavily upon the shoal. There would be no release.

Almost immediately, the noteworthy ship broke in two, steel snapping like twigs. A huge hole had been smashed into her bow, and water entered quickly. The experienced officers and crew were stranded on the forward half containing the pilot house without lifeboats, while on the aft, the galley staff, passengers, and engine crew gathered. Lifeboats were hastily lowered into the restless seas from the stern, but the men forward had no way of reaching the boats.

Of the four women on board, one was the cook's wife and the others were passengers. One of these passengers, Kate Spencer, later told her story to the press: "I cannot think of talk of the wreck without shudder following shudder. At about 6:00 came the terrible crash which broke the vessel in two. We got into the lifeboats at that time, but the captain and the other men could not come aft owing to the break. He hailed us through the megaphone, 'Hang on as long as you can.' We did so but the sea was pounding us so hard that Chief Engineer Phillipi finally directed us out of the small boat and into the large vessel again, all congregating into the dining room which was still intact. The big boat was pounding and tossing. Now a piece of the deck would go of the dining room. During all this time, the men could not get to us. Everything seemed to be breaking up at once, and by order of the Chief Engineer we took to the small boat again. One by one we piled into the small boat leaving six men behind us [on the stern]. I never heard such a heart rending cry as came from those six. 'For God's sake, don't leave us!' they cried. So two of our men got out and helped the six pull the port boat over to the starboard side and launch it. Then we both set out. It was a terrible fight to keep the small boat afloat!'"

The steamer, SEVONA, was noble and noteworthy. Captain McDonald was an esteemed master and as experienced a sailor as could be found on the Great Lakes. Their careers intertwined and they became part of history together. AUTHOR'S COLLECTION.

The Chief Engineer's lifeboat made a daring, but unsuccessful attempt to rescue the men on the bow. Six hours later, after constant struggle to keep afloat, the two lifeboats with 17 people in them came ashore, one on Sand Island and the other at Little Sand Bay.

Rocket flares were launched amidst the ship's continuous whistle blowing, but there was no help that could reach them. The lighthouse keeper at Sand Island helplessly watched the drama through his binoculars.

Captain McDonald, the two mates, two wheelsmen, and two watchmen, all trapped on the bow section, perished in their attempts to reach Sand Island on the flimsy life raft they desperately constructed from several of *Sevona's* hatch covers. Ironically, during *Sevona's* rebuild in the past year, the forward lifeboat had been temporarily removed, but never replaced.

Captain Donald Sutherland McDonald had cheated death once before, several years earlier, when he and another man were the only survivors in a shipwreck off Ireland's coast. Death would not be cheated again. The bodies were recovered. The $1,500 of company money in Captain McDonald's pocket, however, was missing. When "undesirables" began spending watersoaked bills freely in nearby stores and saloons, three were arrested. Charges were dismissed when the prosecuting attorney failed to show up.

After the storm, the SEVONA'S *hull was in shambles, only the stern mast and some davits were left standing, and seven men were dead. A mere 100' of the after end was all that remained of this 372' steel ship.* GREAT LAKES MARINE COLLECTION OF THE MILWAUKEE PUBLIC LIBRARY/WISCONSIN MARINE HISTORICAL SOCIETY.

A month later, the Reid Wrecking Company of Sarnia, Ontario, bought the rights to the wreck for $5,000, and removed portions of it over the next three years, including the three boilers, valued at $10,000 each. In 1909, the U.S. Army Corps of Engineers dynamited what was left of the wreck because it posed a threat to navigation.

Launched as the *Emily P. Weed* in 1890 at West Bay City, Michigan, by F.W. Wheeler & Company, this 2,362-gross-ton steel steamer was propelled by a 1,560 horsepower triple expansion steam engine and three Scotch boilers. The ship was renamed *Sevona* in 1897, eight years before her demise.

The popular wreck of the *Sevona* today lies scattered over a wide area in shallow water to a depth of 20', with the 120' bow piece lying at the southern part of the debris field, and the 230' stern section on the western side. Steel keel, keelson, stringers, frames, and beams lie scattered amidst mounds of iron ore cargo. A *Sevona* anchor is on display at the Little Sand Bay Visitors' Center.

Southwest
(#23 on the map on p. 355)

VESSEL NAME:	SOUTHWEST
RIG:	two-masted schooner
DIMENSIONS:	137' 2" x 26' 1" x 11'
LAUNCHED:	1866; Ogdensburg, New York
DATE LOST:	Sunday, September 18, 1898
CAUSE OF LOSS:	stranded
CARGO:	stone
LIVES LOST:	none (from 8 on board)
GENERAL LOCATION:	SE of Huron Island, Marquette, Michigan
DEPTH:	89' - 111'
ACCESS:	boat
DIVING SKILL LEVEL:	intermediate-advanced
DIVING HAZARDS:	depth, hypothermia, disorientation
CO-ORDINATES:	Lat/Lon: 46.56.42 / 87.56.11
	Loran:

The 137', two-masted schooner, *Southwest,* official number 22359, was built and launched in 1866 at Ogdensburg, New York, constructed by H.C. Pierson. The ship's first enrollment was issued at Chicago, Illinois, on May 18, 1866.

The *Southwest* experienced several mishaps during her long career, including being struck by lightning on Lake Superior in late August, 1880. Only her sails were damaged. Two years later, downbound with a load of iron ore, the *Southwest* was purposely stranded in shallow water at Grand Island, near Munising, Michigan, after she sprang a leak. She was raised and recovered, but her repair set her owner back $3,500. As this wooden vessel aged, she undoubtedly underwent numerous repairs and other maintenance work. One such event was briefly reported in the DETROIT FREE PRESS on September 15, 1894: "The schooner *Southwest* is in Gilmore's drydock at Toledo, having her bottom calked [sic]."

At the age of 32, the *Southwest's* time had run out. On September 19, 1898, while heading upbound to load a cargo of stone at Portage Lake, Michigan, the empty schooner stranded on Huron Island in Lake Superior and sank. No lives were lost. Captain James Gibson and his crew of seven escaped the sinking ship in their yawl boat, landing on the mainland near Skanee. The next day, the steamer, *City of Marquette,* conveyed them to Marquette,

Michigan, where Captain Gibson promptly complained about smoke from the forest fires filling the sky, plus the lack of fog signals on the water, being the causes of accidents. Captain Gibson had a right to be upset. The *Southwest* was not insured.

This was the same forest fire smoke that caused the steamer, *Colorado*, to run aground at Sawtooth Reef off the Keweenaw Peninsula at about the same time.

The *Southwest's* final enrollment was surrendered at Cleveland, Ohio, on February 7, 1899.

The schooner, SOUTHWEST (137' 2" x 26' 1" x 11'), resembled this vessel, the twin-masted schooner, ONEIDA (138' 6" x 24' x 9'), which was built in 1857 at Ashtabula, Ohio, abandoned in 1917 at Green Bay and broken up in the 1920's at Sturgeon Bay, WI. Few, if any, photographs of the SOUTHWEST exist.   AUTHOR'S COLLECTION.

The remains of the schooner, *Southwest,* lie in 88' to 110' of water about a mile southeast of Huron Island, off Marquette, Michigan, in the Marquette Underwater Preserve. They are, for the most part, broken up, but many small items of interest can be seen at this site.

Tioga

(#24 on the map on p. 355)

VESSEL NAME:	TIOGA
RIG:	iron package steamer
DIMENSIONS:	285' 5" x 38' 9" x 25' 7"
LAUNCHED:	Wednesday, December 3, 1884; Buffalo, NY
DATE LOST:	Wednesday, November 26, 1919
CAUSE OF LOSS:	stranded
CARGO:	wheat
LIVES LOST:	none (from 25 on board)
GENERAL LOCATION:	3 miles east of Eagle River, Keweenaw Pen.
DEPTH:	28' - 35'
ACCESS:	boat
DIVING SKILL LEVEL:	novice
DIVING HAZARDS:	minimal
CO-ORDINATES:	Lat/Lon: 47.26.31 / 88.16.21
	Loran: 31817.3 / 46556.3

The five-year-old *Tioga* made headlines not just around the Great Lakes, but across the country, and prompted lawsuits and arguments for months after she exploded at a Chicago dock on July 11, 1890, killing approximately 21 people. Somehow, her cargo of naphtha had caught on fire. The resulting explosion was so powerful that some of the bodies were never found.

This, in a nutshell, is the iron steamer, *Tioga's*, main claim to infamy. She was obviously rebuilt after this tragic, damaging incident. However, when the ship finally sank 29 years later, there were few headlines. Several reasons can be given for this. Firstly, the *Tioga* suffered no loss of life at her demise. Secondly, she was on old (34 years old) ship of a class that was considered obsolete by 1919. Thirdly, newspapers around the Great Lakes were engulfed in the tragic, dramatic story of the loss of the steamer, *Myron,* with 17 of 18 people on board perishing (see pp. 427-434). Any brief mention of the *Tioga's* problems was relegated to a buried page.

The 285', 2,320-gross-ton *Tioga*, launched on December 3, 1884, at Buffalo, New York, kept the same name throughout her long career. She did, however, change owners several times: the Union Steamboat Company of Buffalo (1885-1896), the Erie Railroad Company of Buffalo (1896-1916), the Great Lakes Transit Corporation of Buffalo (1916-1917), and lastly, the Massey Steamship Company of Superior, Wisconsin (1917-1919). It has already been conjectured that it was the move north from Lake Erie to Lake Superior that killed the *Tioga*.

The 285' iron steamer, TIOGA, *built at Buffalo, New York, in 1885, ran aground and broke up with a cargo of wheat off the Keweenaw Peninsula on November 25, 1919. No lives were lost.* REV. PETER VAN DER LINDEN COLLECTION.

On November 26, 1919, three miles east of Eagle River, Michigan, the *Tioga* stranded while struggling through powerful winds and a blizzard. The ship was loaded with grain bound from Superior, Wisconsin, to Buffalo, New York. The vessel's iron hull and double bottom construction failed to keep the vicious elements of Sawtooth Reef at bay. Eight feet of water entering through breaks in the iron hull inundated the engine room and quickly extinguished its source of heat. The crew was trapped for hours at the mercy of the freezing gales and threatening icewater, at one point huddling together for body warmth. Captain Haynie and his crew of 24 were, after several attempts, were safely removed from the doomed ship by the nearby Coast Guard team. The *Tioga*, however, broke up and became a complete loss. Surprisingly, in view of the ship's age, she was valued at over $100,000, while her large cargo of 111,000 bushels of grain was listed at $250,000.

The wooden pilot house from the *Tioga* survived the stranding relatively intact and has been used for many years at Eagle River as a summer cabin, a playhouse, and, for a while, as a craft shop.

The wreck of the *Tioga* has been flattened over the years by the forces of nature, particularly strong and harsh in the Superior northland. Her machinery and boilers, however, are still in place and in very good condition, offering photogenic underwater scenery at this site. The occasional lake trout adds local color.

Vienna (deck level) (#25 on the map on p. 355)

VESSEL NAME:	VIENNA
RIG:	wooden bulk freighter
DIMENSIONS:	191' 4" x 33' 8" x 14' 1"
LAUNCHED:	Thursday, June 19, 1873; Cleveland, Ohio
DATE LOST:	Saturday, September 17, 1892
CAUSE OF LOSS:	collision
CARGO:	iron ore
LIVES LOST:	none
GENERAL LOCATION:	off Whitefish Point, Michigan
DEPTH:	118' - 148'
ACCESS:	boat
DIVING SKILL LEVEL:	advanced
DIVING HAZARDS:	depth, penetration, silting, darkness
CO-ORDINATES:	Lat/Lon: 46.44.46 / 84.57.91
	Loran: 31135.8 / 47610.2

The wreck of the wooden steamer, *Vienna,* is one of the more popular scuba dive sites within the 376 square miles of the Whitefish Point Underwater Preserve in northern Michigan.

Launched on June 19, 1873, at Cleveland, Ohio, by builders Quayle & Martin, the wooden, propeller-driven steamer, *Vienna,* measured 191' 4" in length, 33' 8" in beam, and 14' 1" in draft. The *Vienna* was one of four steamers built for the Cleveland Transportation Company, the others being the *Geneva,* the *Havana,* and the *Sparta,* and they often towed the schooner-barges, *Verona, Genoa, Helena,* and *Sumatra.* The *Vienna's* initial gross tonnage was 745, but this increased to 1,005 when the vessel was double-decked in the spring of 1876.

For nineteen years, the *Vienna,* official number 25875, plied the waters of the Great Lakes with few incidents, working mainly in the iron ore and coal trade, and usually towing the *Verona.*

On Friday, September 16, 1892, the *Vienna,* loaded with iron ore and towing the schooner, *Mattie C. Bell,* similarly cargoed, departed Marquette, Michigan, heading east towards the locks at Sault Ste. Marie, towards Lake Huron. At midnight, with fair weather and clear conditions, the *Vienna* passed Whitefish Point. Captain Nicholson knew that they would reach the Sault locks within two hours, and that the shipping lane would become narrower as he neared those locks.

What happened a few minutes later, at precisely 12:25 A.M., Saturday, September 17, 1892, was never satisfactorily explained. An upbound steamer, the 191-foot, 626-ton *Nipigon,* which had emerged from the Sault locks and was heading out into the open waters of Lake Superior towing the two schooners, *Melbourne* and *Delaware,* had whistled to the *Vienna* that the two steamers should keep each other to their port sides, the regular encountering position. The *Vienna* acknowledged this communication.

The two steamers seemed to be passing each other well, but the next instant, they collided with a terrible crash, the *Nipigon* striking the *Vienna* on the latter's port side. They were about four miles downbound from Whitefish Point, the nearest land. The *Nipigon's* stem and forefoot were badly crushed, but she was not leaking too much. The *Vienna,* however, had received a mortal blow.

Both steamers immediately cut loose the vessels they were towing, leaving their crews to fend for themselves. Captain May of the *Nipigon* ordered that the fatally wounded *Vienna* be taken in tow, and headed for the nearest land, namely Whitefish Point. If the *Vienna* had to sink, it might as well be in the shallows to increase the chances of successful salvage later.

They almost made it. The *Nipigon* towed the *Vienna* for an hour as she increasingly filled with water and became much more difficult to tow. The *Vienna* was hauled to within a mile of shore when the doomed steamer sank. The *Vienna's* crew, having gathered their personal effects, jumped aboard the *Nipigon* as their vessel sank. All were saved. They arrived at Sault Ste. Marie at 4:00 A.M. on board the *Nipigon.* There, the tug, *Merrick,* was sent out to pick up the schooner, *Mattie C. Bell,* while the Nipigon's two tows were lying at safe anchorage just below Whitefish Point.

The *Vienna,* worth $52,000 in 1875, was valued at $40,000 at the time of her loss in 1892, with her cargo appraised at $14,000, sums with far greater purchasing power than they would have today. The *Vienna* belonged to Cleveland's Orient Transportation Company, and was partially insured. Her final enrollment was surrendered at Cleveland, Ohio, on September 28, 1892.

Local newspapers blared the news that the *Vienna* had sunk in 60 fathoms (360 feet) of water, and that nothing could be seen of the vessel above water (steamers in those days had to carry at least two masts and sets of sails in case of power failure to meet insurance requirements; this demand for masts was withdrawn by the underwriters beginning in the year the *Vienna* sank: 1892). Considering the nature of deep Lake Superior, it was certainly possible to be in water 360 feet deep only a mile off shore. However, this was not the case here. Fortunately for sport scuba divers today, the *Vienna's* upper portions rest within the recommended sport diving depth limit of 130 feet.

The 191' wooden steamer, VIENNA, *is pictured at Escanaba, Michigan, with the 190'
schooner-barge,* JOSEPH PAIGE, *ahead of her.* GREAT LAKES MARINE COLLECTION OF
THE MILWAUKEE PUBLIC LIBRARY/WISCONSIN MARINE HISTORICAL SOCIETY.

Scuba divers Kent Bellrichard and Tom Farnquist located the wreck of
the *Vienna* in 1974. The vessel sits upright in 148 feet of water, with the top
deck rising to a depth of 118 feet. The highlights of a *Vienna* exploration can
easily be seen and appreciated without descending deeper than 130 feet. Because
this is Lake Superior, the water visibility is the best in the Great Lakes: 40 to
50 feet is common in the summertime, and even greater in the colder water
months of May and June.

As is the case with most of the shipwrecks in the Whitefish Point
Underwater Preserve, a marker buoy is attached to the *Vienna* with heavy-duty
line every spring, and removed before the ice sets in during the late fall.

The descent to this shipwreck places visiting scuba divers at the wooden
steamer's graceful, curved stern railing. On the stern deck, shovels, axes, and
other tools from over a century ago invite wide-eyed guests to explore further. A
capstan, a mechanical device which made hauling up anchors and other items
easier, appears to guard the approach to the engine and boiler like a short soldier
on duty, or a large-eyed E.T. contemplating home. Numerous lumps of coal
surround the capstan's base, offering proof that one is approaching the coal-fed
engine and boiler, which are huge and magnificent, dwarfing any aquatic callers
who place themselves in this other-era setting. Nearby is a horseshoe, possibly
brought on board with strong hopes for good luck.

IN THE DEPTHS

The Steambarge Vienna Sunk in Sixty Fathoms of Water Near White-fish Point.

Was Run Into by the Nepigon in a Clear Light Early This Morning.

The Crew Saved by Jumping Aboard the Nepigon as the Vienna Went Down.

Nothing Can Now be Seen of the Vessel, Which Was Ore Laden.

SAULT STE. MARIE, Mich., Sept. 17.—[Special to The Herald.]—The steam barge Nepigon, Capt. A. C. May, up bound light towing the schooners Melbourne and Delaware, and the Vienna,

Headlines and subheads in the DULUTH EVENING HERALD *newspaper on September 17, 1892, announcing the loss of the steamer,* VIENNA.

Through a large, open hatchway near the stern, experienced divers may carefully penetrate the below-deck area, where a workbench with a vice attached to it can be studied on the port side. Also below deck at the stern are capstan bars still in place on the wall, as well as two heads (privies).

Back on deck, one of the highlights of this shipwreck is the lifeboat. Originally located years ago on the lake bottom near the *Vienna,* this lifeboat was moved back onto the mother ship by early scuba divers visiting this site.

Below deck on the VIENNA, *at about the 130' depth, diver Joyce Hayward photographs crockery pieces and a vice mounted to a work table.* PHOTO BY CRIS KOHL.

At the heavily damaged bow, a smaller capstan lies on its side.

The *Vienna* is usually buoyed with two markers, the one closer to shore being tied to the steamer's stern.

Part of the legendary "Lake Superior Shipwreck Coast," Whitefish Point offers the most unpredictable weather in the entire Great Lakes system. That, in a nutshell, is the main reason for so many shipwrecks abounding here. Use that as a caution when you go boating in this area.

Scuba charter boat services are available at Whitefish Point harbor, or through the two scuba dive shops in the nearby town of Paradise, Michigan.

Coincidentally, the only museum dedicated solely to shipwrecks in the Great Lakes is at Whitefish Point in the former lighthouse structures which have been restored to their prime glory. The Great Lakes Shipwreck Historical Museum, located at the tip of Whitefish Point at the end of the road from Paradise, offers glimpses of archival photos, ship's models, restored artifacts, and underwater videotapes of many of the shipwrecks in this area. It is an excellent place to visit between scuba dives or after a day of diving.

ABOVE: *The stern capstan, one of the first sights to greet visiting divers who descend at the* VIENNA'S *stern, gazes across the decking like an extraterrestrial, with coal, silt, and other debris at its feet.* BELOW: *In 1984, curious divers explored the lake bottom off the* VIENNA'S *hull, located one of her lifeboats, and returned it to the ship. It sits on the starboard side between midship and stern.* PHOTOS BY CRIS KOHL.

APPENDIX D

The 100 Most Hunted Great Lakes Shipwrecks

Shipwreck hunting has always been a thrilling adventure. Two or three hundred years ago, it was done to recover gold, silver, and jewels that went down with the ship, which made it profitable as well as exciting. This sort of activity was virtually limited to the tropics, since no treasure fleets succumbed to hurricanes on the Great Lakes. Indeed, the first shipwrecks on these inland seas did not occur until 1679 (and the beaver pelts on board would not stay preserved like Spanish galleon treasures). Great Lakes shipwrecks occurred very sparingly until the end of the War of 1812. Our history of shipwrecks is quite youthful, innocent, and perhaps a tad lackluster in comparison to that of the Caribbean.

One hundred years ago, shipwreck hunting was done to salvage whatever cargo happened to be on board. This applied to most shipwrecks in most parts of the world, since hardhat diving was firmly entrenched as a dangerous, but glorious and potentially lucrative profession. Salvage in the Great Lakes consisted chiefly in recovering coal, iron ore, grain, or lumber cargoes, or in attempting to raise the entire sunken vessel and restoring it to service. A very few dramatic exceptions included the 1856 raising of the trunk containing $36,000 from the Lake Erie wreck of the paddlewheeler, *Atlantic*. Great Lakes salvagers, or "wreckers," were an élite group of daring men (and one woman) involved in a recognized, accepted profession, members of a distinct minority which received considerable respect and publicity for its hazardous calling. From a business point of view, these people worked in a "feast or famine" setting, with one good salvage job often providing quite comfortable livelihoods for a year or two. However, if their attempts at salvage failed, they often lost money in the venture, since they usually worked on a "no cure, no pay" basis.

Today on the Great Lakes, shipwreck hunting is done for totally different reasons. Shipwrecks are recognized by many individuals, as well as state and provincial governments, as having irreplaceable historic significance, so the profession of "wrecking" as it existed a hundred years ago has become obsolete. With a greater sensitivity to recognizing our past, we have become aware that there are gaps and footnotes in Great Lakes history crying out to be filled. More and more, we want the complete story, the puzzles solved entirely about the ships which plied the waters of these inland seas and succumbed to them. Locating a shipwreck helps put closure to an often tragic mystery, and on a local level, this could be as dramatic as the effect that the finding of Amelia Earhart's longlost aircraft would have upon the world.

The finding of a shipwreck should not be shrugged off as an everyday, an easy, or an insignificant accomplishment. We reached the moon 16 years before we found the *Titanic!* Think about it.

Also, with the rapid growth of scuba diving's popularity since World War II, we want to see and personally touch these authentic museum pieces which often represent an era totally foreign to us and beyond our grasp today. Perhaps there is underlying nostalgia for those long-gone times, represented by these shipwrecks, when life was simpler, slower, and physically more challenging. With scuba equipment, we can get back to the place, but not the time. Our knowledge of lakes history, and our imaginations, fill in from there.

Often Great Lakes shipwrecks are found accidentally. A commercial fishing boat might snag a net on an underwater obstruction and contact a diver to free and recover their valuable net. Sometimes nets have come up with rust marks on them, a near-certain sign that a steel shipwreck lies below. On some occasions, shipwreck parts, such as anchors, have snagged and been raised along with the net. With the profusion of electronically well-equipped powerboats in the past 20 years, several recreational boaters have inadvertently found shipwrecks simply by passing over them with their fishfinder or depthsounder suddenly displaying an anomaly, or dramatic rise, from the lake bottom.

There is also a handful of determined, adventurous Great Lakes shipwreck locaters who do considerable historical research prior to spending days at a time patiently and slowly "mowing the water" in pre-ascertained areas with their boats and whatever equipment they are using to find shipwrecks: sidescan sonars, proton magnetometers, surplus World War II submarine detection equipment, fishfinders, dragging cables, dragging divers, or whatever. These people are aware of the historical significance of Great Lakes shipwrecks, plus the fact that they themselves are adding to the history of a shipwreck by finding it.

Generally speaking, the most sought shipwrecks are those with historic significance and those most likely to be found in as intact a condition as possible. Those which foundered in a storm or from a leaking condition are usually in very good shape when they are found. Ships which sank due to a collision are also sought, since their damage is usually minimal or confined to one specific area. Ships which burned to the waterline and sank are often in poor shape, while ships which stranded on rocks often broke into too many pieces to make them identifiable. The following shipwrecks are the ones that have been searched for already, but have not yet been located, or shipwrecks which will likely be in very good condition when they are found.

Lake Ontario Shipwrecks

BARNES, BURT --- This three-masted schooner (95'5" x 24'5" x 7'3") sank somewhere south of Point Traverse, Ontario, on September 2, 1926, some time after the crew escaped in a lifeboat. All the masts had snapped. This beautiful ship, carrying a cargo of coal when lost, was built at Manitowoc, WI, in 1882.

BARNES, FRANK C. --- This wooden tug (66'7" x 16'3" x 7'2") foundered with the loss of all hands (5) on November 1, 1915, off Salmon Point, Ontario. This ship was built at Manistee, Michigan, in 1892.

BERMUDA --- This 115' schooner, built by John Tait and launched in June, 1867, at Robbins Mills, Ontario, foundered off Port Granby, Ontario, on November 6, 1880. The crew "had most narrow escapes, the boat being swamped."

BOSTON --- This wooden steamer (133'8" x 20'10" x 9'9"), built at Cleveland, Ohio, in 1847 by Luther Moses, sank after a collision with the bark, PLYMOUTH, off Oak Orchard, New York, on July 28, 1854.

CARTER, W.J. --- This wooden lumber hooker (122' x 28' x 9'6"), built at Milwaukee, WI, in 1886, sank with a cargo of coal enroute from Oswego, NY to Cobourg, ON, after springing a leak about 20 miles south of Point Petre, Ontario, on July 28, 1923. A lifeboat saved the eight men and one woman.

GRAMMAR, NISBET --- On May 31, 1926, this steel steamer (253' x 43' 5" x 20'), built at Birkenhead, England, in 1923, sank with no lives lost within 15 minutes after a collision with the steamer, DALWARNIC, in fog off Thirty Mile Point, New York, near Charlotte (Rochester) while loaded with grain for Montreal.

HALL, JOHN E. --- This wooden steamer (139' x 28'6" x 10' 9"), built at Manitowoc, WI, in 1889, foundered near the Duck Islands off Point Traverse, Ontario, on December 14, 1902, with the loss of all hands (9) and a cargo of coal.

HIAWATHA --- This wooden, multi-masted towbarge (176'5" x 30' x 11'9"), built at Garden Island, ON, near Kingston, in 1890, foundered on September 20, 1917, 8 miles off Yorkshire Island in the Ducks. Only the captain survived.

HORN, CHARLES --- This wooden steamer (202'2" x 34'7" x 13'1"), built as the MARION in 1889 at Sheboygan, WI, burned and sank with a grain cargo when 26 miles off Point Petre Light on May 16, 1926; no lives were lost.

JESKA --- This small composite steamer (123'6" x 23'6" x 12'), built at Kingston, Ontario, in 1909, foundered during a gale on October 7, 1926 about ten miles off Fair Haven, New York, in about 300' of water. No lives were lost.

JEX, H.N. --- Launched as the LAWRENCE in 1868 at Cleveland, OH, this wooden steamer (170'2" x 26'5" x 10'3") foundered on August 16, 1921, 10 miles SE of Point Petre or Long Point, ON, with a coal cargo and no loss of life.

MOIRA --- This steamer (123' x 25'), built at Belleville, Ontario, in 1855, leaked and sank south of Main Duck Island on October 9, 1862, reportedly in 50' or 70'. All were saved in the lifeboats. Lost with the ship was the cargo of coal, general merchandise, passengers' personal property, and a horse.

MOORE, JOHN --- This wooden barge (119'7" x 38'6" x 8'5"), built at Port Colborne, ON, in 1911, foundered on April 21, 1940, 6 miles east of the Eastern Gap at Toronto, and 3 miles from shore.

NEW YORK, CITY OF --- Launched at Cleveland, OH, in August, 1863, this wooden steamer (136' x 27'6" x 11'6") foundered with all hands (8) during a snowstorm on November 25, 1921, between Main Duck and Galloo Islands.

NORTHWEST --- The bow half of this huge steel freighter sank on November 29, 1918, with the loss of two lives. The ship (358' x 44' x 23'), built at Cleveland, Ohio, in 1894, had been cut in half for transport through the old Welland Canal for use in Europe in World War I. One report states that it sank 7 miles off Prince Edward County, Ontario, while another gives its depth at 100'.

The steel steamer, NORTHWEST, as it appeared in HARPER'S WEEKLY, 1894.

ROBERVAL --- This steel steamer (128' x 24' x 8'), built at Toronto in 1907, foundered in a storm about 12 miles off Oswego, NY, on September 25, 1916.

SHANNON --- This small schooner (78' x 19' x 6') foundered after springing a leak about 18 miles off Oswego, NY, on June 20, 1874, with no lives lost.

SPEEDY --- This historic schooner (about 80' x 20' x 7'), built at Kingston, ON, in 1798, sank with all hands (20-27) in a storm 4 miles off Presqu'isle, ON, on October 8, 1804, with the loss of prominent people and an accused murderer. Claims to this wreck's discovery have not been substantiated.

WAFFLE, J.T. --- This small, wooden steamer (105' x 23' x 8'), launched at Westport, ON, in 1914, foundered with all hands (8) and a load of coal on September 22, 1919, somewhere between Oswego, NY, and the Ducks Islands, ON.

WARREN, HOMER --- Built as the wooden passenger ship, ATLANTIC, at Cleveland, OH, in 1863, this steamer (177' x 30' x 12') foundered with all hands (8) and a cargo of coal on October 28, 1919, off Putneyville, NY.

Lake Erie Shipwrecks

ATLANTIS --- This fish tug (47' x 14'7" x 4'3") launched as the DESPATCH in 1916 at Erie, PA, foundered in a storm off Erieau, ON, on November 21, 1958.

BATES, ELI --- Lost with all hands (9) without a trace on Nov. 16, 1871, 7 miles north of Ashtabula, OH, this 265-ton schooner was built at Erie, PA, in 1857.

BLACK MARLIN --- Foundered with no lives lost on Nov. 29, 1958, off Avon Point, OH, along with the derrick scow HICKORY STICK, this wooden fish tug (39'8" x 13'8" x 3'5") was launched as the MARTHA M. at Vermilion, OH, in 1935.

CARR, HONORA --- This schooner (92' x 23' x 8'), built as the MAPLE LEAF at Picton, ON, in 1867, foundered near Buffalo, NY, on September 4, 1886; 1 life lost.

CELTIC --- This wooden steamer (131' x 21' x 14' 7"), built at Hamilton, ON, in 1874, sank with wheat, general cargo, and 1 life lost after colliding with the steamer, RUSSIA, in fog about 15 miles off Rondeau, ON, on May 1, 1892.

COMMODORE --- This 1880 schooner-barge (176'5" x 34' x 12'2") foundered 10-20 miles off the SE Shoal Light off Point Pelee, ON, on June 17, 1918, while in tow of the steamer, JAY GOULD, which also sank. No lives were lost.

CORNELL --- Built as the GRACE DANFORTH at Buffalo, NY, in 1888, this tug (72' x 17'4" x 10') foundered mysteriously in mild weather with all hands (8) on December 21, 1922, somewhere between Cleveland, OH, and Erie, PA.

COURTLAND --- This 3-masted bark (173'6" x 34'4" x 13'8"), built in 1867, sank in a collision with the paddlewheeler, MORNING STAR, 21 miles NNE of Vermilion, OH, on June 21, 1868, with the loss of 7 lives from the bark.

FILER, D.L. --- Lost with 6 of 7 on board in the Black Friday Storm of Oct. 20, 1916, 3 miles east of Bar Point Light near the mouth of the Detroit River, this schooner-barge (156'6" x 30' x 10') was built in 1871 at Manistee, MI.

KENT --- This much-sought 122' steamer, built at Chatham, ON (then Canada West) in 1841, sank in about 67' of water after a collision with the steamer, LONDON, off Point Pelee on Aug. 12, 1845, with the loss of coins and about 10 lives.

KILLARNEY --- Built in 1929 at Mariners Harbor, New York, as the SOCONY 23, this tug (91'5" x 22' x 10') sank on September 12, 1974, 20 miles off Fairport, OH, with no loss of life. One reported position is 42.06N x 81.10W.

LEXINGTON --- This small, 53-ton schooner sank in a storm with all hands (13) four miles off Pt. Mouillee, MI, (another report puts her 5-10 miles off Huron, OH!) on November 19, 1846. The cargo of 110 barrels of whiskey turned this wreck into a legend, but most of those barrels washed ashore in 1846.

LOGAN, ELIZA --- Launched in 1855 at Buffalo, NY, this schooner (130'6" x 28'1" x 11') foundered 16 miles off Erie, PA on October 19, 1871, with 2 lives lost.

MAGNETIC --- This four-masted schooner-barge (264'1" x 38'5" x 19'9"), loaded with iron ore, broke in two and sank 19 miles west of Long Point, ON, on August 25, 1917, with no lives lost. She was built at Cleveland, OH, in 1882.

MARQUETTE & BESSEMER #2 --- Long-elusive, much-hyped, and prematurely-claimed-as-found, this steel railroad car ferry (338' x 54' x 19'5"), Cleveland-built in 1905, foundered on December 8, 1909, with all hands (31-38) somewhere between Port Stanley, Ontario, and Conneaut, Ohio. Lots of searchers.

OAKLAND --- This wooden steamer (184' x 28'8" x 9'8"), built at Erie, PA, in 1868, foundered off Conneaut, OH, September 16, 1883, with a lumber cargo.

PICTON --- This 1870 paddlewheel steamer (158' x 26' x 8'), built at Mill Point, ON, stranded just offshore Rondeau, ON, on September 22, 1882; no lives lost.

SHICKLUNA, L. --- Five miles east of Long Point, ON, this wooden steamer (135' x 26' x 12'), built in St. Catharines, ON, in 1870, sank in a collision on April 28, 1897.

VANDALIA ---This steamer (91' x 18') was one of the first propeller-driven vessels on the Great Lakes. Launched at Oswego, NY, in 1841, this ship sank after a collision with the schooner, FASHION, on Oct. 27, 1851, west of Pt. Pelee.

VENICE, CITY OF --- This 1892 wooden steamer (301' x 42'5" x 20'1"), built at West Bay City, MI, sank after a collision with the steamer, SEGUIN, off Rondeau, ON, on August 4, 1902. Three lives were lost. The wreck was dynamited.

Lake Huron Shipwrecks

ASIA --- This wooden steamer (136' x 23'4" x 11'), built at St. Catharines, ON, in 1873, foundered in Georgian Bay off Byng Inlet, ON, on September 14, 1882, with 123 lives lost and two survivors. A much sought shipwreck.

ATHENS --- Built at West Bay City, MI, in 1897, this schooner-barge (310' x 45' x 20') broke in two and sank on October 7, 1917, 25 miles west of Southampton, ON. Five of eight people on board perished.

BRUCE MINES --- This 126' sidewheel steamer foundered in a storm off Cape Hurd near Tobermory, ON, on November 28, 1854, with one life lost. This ship, built at Montreal in 1842, reportedly sank in 70 fathoms (420') of water.

BURNS, ROBERT --- This 127' brig, built at Port Huron, MI, in 1848, foundered east of Bois Blanc Island on November 17, 1869, with 10 lives and wheat lost.

CARRUTHERS, JAMES --- A victim of the Great Storm of November 9, 1913, this new, steel freighter (550' x 58'2" x 26'7"), built at Collingwood, ON, earlier that year, foundered with all hands (22-24) and a wheat cargo off Kincardine, ON.

CLIFTON --- One of the few whalebacks in our Great Lakes, this steamer (308' x 38' x 24'), built at Superior, WI, in 1892, as the SAMUEL MATHER, foundered 25 miles off Thunder Bay, MI, on September 22, 1924, with all hands (24).

COBURN, R.G. --- This one-year-old wooden steamer (193'4" x 30'8" x 8'5"), built at Marine City, MI, in 1870, foundered 20-25 miles off Point Aux Barques, MI, on Oct. 15, 1871, with 31 lives lost from 49. Wheat, flour, silver ore.

A few of the dozens of successful Great Lakes shipwreck researchers, hunters, and explorers are (clockwise from lower left): David Trotter of Canton, Michigan, who has found scores of shipwrecks and produced numerous slide shows on them; John Steele of Waukegan, Illinois, and Kent Bellrichard of Milwaukee, Wisconsin, eyeing the sidescan sonar unit while searching for the A.A. PARKER in Lake Superior. Between the two of them, they have found a hundred shipwrecks; and Mike Fletcher of Port Dover, Ontario, who located the famous wreck of the ATLANTIC in Lake Erie, pictured here with partner Dennis Barrington and noted marine artist Robert McGreevy, with the latter's original drawing of the ATLANTIC. PHOTOS BY CRIS KOHL.

FRANZ, W.C. --- Sunk in a collision with the steamer, EDWARD E. LOOMIS in fog with 4 lives lost 30 miles SE of Thunder Bay Island, MI, on November 21, 1934, this steel steamer (346' x 48' x 28') was built at Wyandotte, MI, in 1901.

GOODYEAR, FRANK --- This steel steamer (416' x 50' x 28'), launched at Lorain, OH, in 1902, sank with a load of iron ore in a collision with the steamer, JAMES B. WOOD, off Point Aux Barques, MI, on May 23, 1910; 17 of 22 men died.

GRAHAM, JENNIE --- In a storm in mid-April, 1880, this 146' schooner struck a rock and sank south of Great Duck Island. That shoal was named after the ship.

GRIFFON --- The Mount Everest or TITANIC goal of Great Lakes shipwreck hunters, this longlost brig was the first ship on the upper Great Lakes. It mysteriously and dramatically disappeared with all hands (5) on her maiden voyage in September, 1679, and, although 16 locations have argued claims to the GRIFFON'S bones, the strongest case comes from western Manitoulin Island, ON, at the Mississagi Straits. Critics say more evidence is needed.

HYDRUS --- This steel steamer (416' x 50' x 28'), built at Lorain, OH, in 1903, foundered with all hands (24) in the Great Storm of November 9, 1913, off Southampton, Ontario, where bodies and wreckage washed ashore.

JONES, J.H. --- This small, wooden steamer (107' x 21'4" x 9'5") sank with all hands (26) off Cape Croker, Georgian Bay, Ontario, on November 22, 1906. The ship had been built in 1888 at Goderich, Ontario.

KALIYUGA --- Built at St. Clair, MI, in 1887, this wooden steamer (270' x 40' x 21') foundered with all hands (17) and a load of iron ore somewhere between Alpena and Port Huron, MI, in a storm on October 20, 1905.

MILLER, JANE --- Somewhere off the mouth of Colpoy Bay, near Wiarton, ON, in Georgian Bay water probably about 200-250' deep, lies the wreck of this wooden steamer (78' x 18' x 8') which foundered with all hands (30) in a storm on Nov. 26, 1881. The ship was built at Little Current, ON, in 1878.

MILLS, MERRILL I. --- This large tug (121'8" x 20'3" x 10'8") sank off Sand Beach, MI, in a collision with the bark, UNADILLA, on May 9, 1873, reportedly in 15 fathoms (90') of water. The ship was built at Marine City, MI in 1867.

NORTHERNER --- This sidewheel passenger steamer (186'7" x 26'8" x 10'9"), launched at Cleveland in 1851, sank in a collision with the steamer, FOREST QUEEN, with 12 lives lost, on April 16, 1856, 4 miles north of Port Huron, MI.

PESHTIGO --- This 161' schooner, built at Peshtigo, WI, in 1863, sank with a cargo of coal in a collision with the schooner, ST. ANDREW, on June 25, 1878, with two lives lost. The ST. ANDREW has been located, but the PESHTIGO is still missing somewhere about 5 miles west of Cheboygan, MI.

REGINA --- This small, 75' schooner, built in 1866 at St. Catharines, ON, foundered on Sept. 10, 1881, reportedly in 7 fathoms (42') 4 miles off Cove Island or Cove Island Light, near Tobermory, ON, with the loss of her captain.

WEXFORD --- Another victim of the Great Storm of November 9, 1913, lost with all hands (18-22), this steel steamer (250' x 40'1" x 23'7") was built in Sunderland, England, in 1883. Her last known location is off Goderich, ON.

Lake Michigan Shipwrecks

AKELEY, H.C. --- This large, wooden steamer of 1,187 gross tons, built in 1881 at Grand Haven, MI, foundered in a storm on November 13, 1883, with a cargo of corn about 15 miles off Holland, MI, with the loss of 6 lives out of 18.

ALPENA --- This 1867 wooden steamer (197' x 26'8" x 12'), built at Marine City, MI, foundered with all hands (73) about 20 miles off Kenosha, WI, on Oct. 16, 1880, in powerful gales. Wreckage washed ashore near Holland, MI.

ANDASTE --- Foundered in the middle of the lake south of Grand Haven, MI, (also given as 14 miles west of Holland, MI) with all hands (25) on Sept. 9, 1929, this steel steamer (266'9" x 38'1" x 17'9") was launched at Cleveland in 1892.

ARCADIA --- This wooden steamer (118'8" x 26'2" x 9'1"), built at Milwaukee, WI, in 1888, foundered off Ludington, MI, on April 14, 1907, with all hands (14).

CHICORA --- A long-sought shipwreck, this wooden steamer (198'5" x 35' x 13'6"; add 10' for overall length) built at Detroit in 1892, foundered with all hands (26) on January 21, 1895, on a run from Milwaukee to St. Joseph, MI.

The passenger steamer, CHICORA, disappeared on Lake Michigan on January 21, 1895, with the loss of all 26 lives on board. (Samuel Ward Stanton drawings, 1895)

CHURCHILL --- This schooner-barge (202' x 38' x 16'), launched in 1890 at Toledo, OH, foundered in a storm off Waukegan, IL, with 2 lives lost on October 13, 1898.

ELLSWORTH, LEM --- This three-masted schooner (138' x 26' x 11'), built at Milwaukee in 1874, foundered with all hands (7) and a cargo of building stone during a storm on May 23-24, 1894, bound from Jacobsville, MI, to Chicago. Her yawl was found off Waukegan, IL, and another report places her sinking at 2 miles off Kenosha, WI.

GILCHER, W.H. --- One of the first steel steamers (301'5" x 41'2" x 21'1"), built at Cleveland in 1891, she foundered off High Island on October 28, 1892, with all hands (17) lost. She possibly collided with the schooner, OSTRICH. Reported found by Chicago hardhat diver, Frank Blair, on July 12, 1935.

LAC LA BELLE --- Built at Cleveland in 1864 and sunk in the St. Clair River for three years before recovery, this wooden steamer (216'1" x 37'1" x 19'7") ultimately foundered 20 miles off Racine, WI, on October 14, 1872, with 8 lives and a cargo of pork, grain, and flour lost.

LAWRENCE, A.W. --- This tug (72' x 16' x 9'), built at Sturgeon Bay, WI, in 1880, exploded and sank off Milwaukee on October 30, 1888, with 4 lives lost.

MORAN, JOHN V. --- Cut by ice and sunk 20 miles off Muskegon, MI on February 7, 1899, this wooden steamer (214' x 37' x 22'2") was built at West Bay City, MI, in 1888. No lives were lost in this sinking.

NIKO --- This 1889 wooden steamer (189' x 35' x 13'), built at Trenton, MI, bound light for Manistique, MI, sprang a leak and sank in shallow water in a gale off Garden Island, MI (in the Beaver group), on Nov. 2, 1924, no lives lost.

OSTRICH --- Possibly in a collision with the W.H. GILCHER, this schooner (140' x 26' x 11'), sailing light, sank west of the Manitou Islands on October 28, 1892, with the loss of all hands (6). She was built at Buffalo, NY, in 1856.

OUR SON --- This 55-year-old schooner (182'1" x 35'1" x 13'), the last of those built on the Great Lakes, foundered in a storm 20 miles off Sheboygan, WI, with no lives lost on September 26, 1930. She was built at Lorain, OH, in 1875.

PETERS, R.G. --- This 386-ton wooden steamer, built at Milwaukee in 1880, burned and sank in a blinding storm on December 1, 1882, in mid-lake with the loss of all hands (14).

PRINGLE, ROBERT C. --- Waterlogged and sunk off Manitowoc, WI, on July 19, 1922, this tug (101' x 22' x 10') was built in 1903 at Manitowoc.

REDFERN, C.E. --- This motorship (181' x 35' x 13'1"), built as a schooner at West Bay City, MI, in 1890 and converted in 1926, foundered 4 miles off Point Betsie, MI, Light on a heading of 313 degrees, on September 19, 1937, with a load of pulpwood. No lives were lost.

SASSACUS --- This schooner (95' x 22' x 7'), launched at Oswego, NY, in 1867, beached in a storm on Sept. 30, 1893, and was pulled off, but sank while in tow on Oct. 8, 1893, 2 miles north of the east entrance of Sturgeon Bay.

SENATOR --- Sunk in a collision with the steamer, MARQUETTE, on October 31, 1929, in fog 20 miles NE of Port Washington, WI, with 7 of 22 lives lost, this steel steamer (410' x 45'4" x 23'9") was built at Wyandotte, MI, in 1896. She carried 240 Nash automobiles at the time of loss.

WESTMORELAND--- This wooden steamer (202'2" x 28'2" x 12'2"), built at Cleveland in 1853, foundered on December 8, 1854, off South Manitou Island while bound from Chicago to Mackinac Island with flour and provisions; 17 lives were lost. Reportedly also carried liquor, with salvage in 1872 or 1874.

Lake Superior Shipwrecks

ARLINGTON--- This steel steamer (244' x 43' x 18'2"), launched as the *F.P. Jones* at Wyandotte, MI, in 1913, foundered on May 1, 1940, with a wheat cargo near Superior Shoals. The captain alone perished from the 17 on board.

BANNOCKBURN --- Only a lifeboat oar was found 18 months after this steel steamer (245' 1" x 40'1" x 18'4") foundered somewhere in the lake on November 22, 1902, with the loss of all hands (22). Since then, this ship, built in England in 1893, has become the Great Lakes' "Flying Dutchman," reportedly seen afloat several times in the years after she sank.

BARGE 129 --- This steel whaleback barge (292' x 36' x 22') built at Superior, WI, in 1893, sank in a collision with her towing steamer, the MAUNALOA, on Oct. 13, 1902, off Vermilion Pt., MI. No lives were lost, and the wreck reportedly sits in 129' of water.

CERISOLES/INKERMAN --- These two steel French warships (135'6" x 26'2" x 12'7"), just launched at Fort William (now Thunder Bay), Ontario, with modern 100mm cannons mounted at bow and stern, foundered in a storm with all hands (76) somewhere in the lake on November 24, 1918, on their maiden voyages to France. A third sister ship, the SEBASTOPOL, survived this storm.

CHAPPELL, W.T. --- This small, 2-masted 1877 schooner (57'5" x 15'6" x 5") capsized and sank with a wood cargo 4.5 mi. ENE of Vermilion Pt., Whitefish Bay, on Oct. 24, 1902, both crew being rescued. She was built at Sebewaing, MI.

CYPRESS --- Only 25 days old and on her second voyage, this steel steamer (420' x 52' x 28'), built at Lorain, OH, capsized and sank on October 11, 1907, 19 miles off Deer Park, MI, with 21 of 22 lives and a load of iron ore lost.

HULBERT, MARY ANN --- This was the worst sailing ship disaster on the lake, with 20 lives lost when this small, 62-ton schooner-barge, in tow of the steamer, KINCARDINE, foundered in a strong storm on December 14, 1883, 40 miles NE of present-day Thunder Bay, Ontario, off St. Ignace Island.

LAMBTON --- This steel steamer (108' x 25'1" x 12'7"), built at Sorel, Quebec, in 1908, foundered in a gale between Caribou Island and Whitefish Bay on April 19, 1922, with all hands (22), mostly lighthouse keepers.

LEAFIELD --- Lost with all hands (18) in the Great Storm of November 9, 1913, this steel steamer (249' x 35'2" x 16'6"), built at Sunderland, England, in 1892, stranded on Angus Island, 20 miles east of Thunder Bay, ON, with a cargo of steel rails before the storm tore her loose and sank her in about 250'-300'.

MARQUETTE --- This leaking vessel made it to within 5 miles east of Michigan Island, in the Apostle Islands group, with a load of iron ore before breaking in two and foundering on October 15, 1903, with no lives lost. This wooden steamer (235' x 35'7" x 18'5") was built in 1881 at Cleveland.

MISSOULA --- This wooden steamer (272' x 40'6" x 21') foundered with a cargo of wheat in a gale 15 miles NE of Caribou Island on November 2, 1895, with no lives lost. The ship was built in 1887 at Cleveland.

NOBLE, BENJAMIN --- Reportedly foundered off Knife Island on April 27, 1914, with all hands (20), this steel steamer (239'2" x 42'2" x 18'8"), built at Wyandotte, MI, in 1909, carried a cargo of steel rails.

ORINOCO --- This wooden steamer (295' x 44' x 21'), built at West Bay City, MI, in 1898, foundered on May 18, 1924, 6 miles off Agawa Bay, NNW of the Soo, with the loss of 5 lives and a load of pulpwood.

OWEN, JOHN --- Lost in the same gale which sank the MYRON (see pp. 427-434), this composite steamer (281' x 41' x 20'), launched at Wyandotte, MI, in 1889, foundered on November 13, 1919, with all hands (22) and a cargo of grain between Manitou Island and Stannard Rock.

PARKER, A. A. --- Built in 1884 at Cleveland as the KASOTA, this wooden steamer (246'9" x 38'2" x 20'9") leaked and sank with an iron ore cargo a few miles off Grand Marais, MI, on September 19, 1903. The crew was rescued. One source says she sank in 120', but several attempts to find her have failed.

PEREW, FRANK --- This three-masted schooner (174'2" x 30'8" x 13'2"), built at Cleveland in 1867, foundered 15 miles off Whitefish Point on September 29, 1891, with a load of coal and 6 out of 7 crew members lost.

SATELLITE --- This 233-ton tug was towing five ships on June 21, 1879, when it struck a deadhead (floating log) and sank west of Whitefish Point; no loss of life.

SOVEREIGN --- This wooden steamer (139' x 24' 12') sprang a leak and foundered in a severe storm on October 25, 1891, 12 miles SW of Lamb Island Light, with no lives lost. This ship was built at St. Catharines, Ontario, in 1873.

STEELVENDOR --- Lost during World War II with a cargo of steel billets intended for war production, this steel steamer (250'3" x 42'9" x 17'2"), built at Kearney, New Jersey, in 1923, capsized and foundered in huge seas on Sept. 3, 1942, 15 miles east (68 degrees) of Manitou Island, with 1 life lost out of 25.

WESTERN RESERVE --- The first steel steamer (300' 7" x 41'2" x 21') built on the Great Lakes (Cleveland, 1890), she broke in half during a storm and foundered off Deer Park, MI, on August 30, 1892, with 26 out of 27 lives lost. This drew enormous criticism of steel producers and created skepticism for steel ships.

APPENDIX E

200 Shipwrecks in Great Lakes Parks and Preserves

Shipwreck name in **BOLD** lettering indicates one of the "100 best" wrecks.

Unidentified shipwrecks have not been included in these listings.

It is interesting to note that of the "100 best" Great Lakes shipwrecks, 42 of them are in underwater parks or preserves.

Fathom Five National Marine Park
Tobermory, Ontario (Lake Huron)

Fathom Five National Marine Park, established as a provincial park in 1972 and transferred to national park status in 1987, was the first underwater park/preserve created in the Great Lakes. There are 21 known shipwrecks (some unidentified) within five miles of Tobermory, Ontario, inside the boundaries of this park. Each scuba diver visiting here is required to register at the Registration Center prior to diving in the park; boaters must also register. There is a small registration fee, payable only once each calendar year.

ALICE G./JOHN & ALEX/BOB FOOTE/ROBERT K. --- These four tugboats lie so close together just outside Little Tub (Tobermory) Harbor that they are usually explored as a single tank shore dive. The 67' *Alice G.*, the best preserved one, went aground in gale force winds and sank in November, 1927. The 59' fishing tug, *John & Alex,* burned on Saturday, December 6, 1947. The *Bob Foote* sank in 1905, and the 68' *Robert K.* burned on Sunday, June 23, 1935. Their remains lie mostly scattered in 5' to 40' of water. This area is buoyed for divers.

ARABIA --- See *The 100 Best Great Lakes Shipwrecks, Volume I,* pp. 135-138.

AVALON VOYAGER II --- This 135' wooden steamer, built in Newfoundland in 1946, stranded off Cape Hurd on Saturday, October 31, 1981 and eventually became a total loss with no lives lost. The ship was en route to Owen Sound, ON, for use there as a restaurant. The remains, which can be seen from the surface, are badly broken and scattered in up to 25' of water, just off the west end of Bonnet Island near Hay Bay, SW of Tobermory.

BRECK, MARION L. --- Off the pointy south end of Bear's Rump Island, a few miles to the NE of Tobermory, in water 10'-100' deep, lie the broken and scattered remains of this old, 127' schooner, which stranded there on Thursday, November 15, 1900. The entire crew abandoned ship safely. Major portions of this wreck, which is not usually buoyed, lie at 25', 50', 75', and 90'.

CASCADEN --- In water to a depth of 20' lie the broken and scattered remains of this schooner, built in Southampton, ON, in 1866. The ship stranded just to the NE of Cape Hurd on Sunday, October 15, 1871, with the crew surviving.

CHINA --- The 137' schooner, built at Port Robinson, ON, in 1863, wrecked on this reef which now bears her name SW of Tobermory and just SSE of Wreck Point on Tuesday, November 20, 1883, with no loss of lives. The badly broken and scattered wooden wreckage lies in 6'-20' of water.

FOREST CITY --- See *The 100 Best Great Lakes Shipwrecks, Vol. I*, Appendix C: 100 Deep Great Lakes Shipwrecks, p. 244.

GRAND RAPIDS, CITY OF --- Burned in Big Tub Harbour on Tuesday, October 29, 1907, this 123' wooden steamer was built at Grand Haven, MI, in 1879. The wreck, in water to 15' deep, is located about 150' off the starboard bow of the SWEEPSTAKES wreck, can also be seen from the surface easily, and is usually explored in tandem with an exploration of the more popular SWEEPSTAKES. These wrecks are sometimes off-limits to divers because of the glassbottom boats. Check for times at the registration office.

KING, JAMES C. --- This 181' schooner-barge stranded while being towed by the steamer, W.L. WETMORE (which was also wrecked; see p. 477) on November 29, 1901. All on board were saved. The KING lies along a steep incline in 22'-93' of water off the western tip of Russel Island. Her bow lies deepest, and her rudder, in about 20' of water, can be seen from the surface; the wreck site, like most of those in this park, is buoyed during the tourist season.

MINCH, CHARLES P. --- Built at Vermilion, OH, in 1867, this 154' three-masted schooner was destroyed in a storm while hauling lumber on October 26, 1898, along the south shore of Tecumseh Cove on the SE side of Cove Island, just north of Tobermory. No lives were lost. Large and small sections of hull and planking lie in 20'-55' of water in two main areas, one by the cribs and the other buoyed.

NEWAYGO --- This 196' wooden steamer, built at Marine City, MI, in 1890, stranded and broke up on Northwest Bank, Devil Island Channel, west of Tobermory, on November 17, 1903, with no lives lost. The wreckage is widely scattered in 20'-25' of water at this open site.

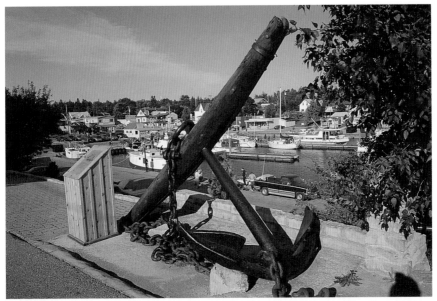

ABOVE: *The town of Tobermory, Ontario, has changed considerably since I first photographed its harbor with fishing nets drying on racks in 1966. This picture, showing an anchor from the* CHARLES P. MINCH *and the town's harbor, is from the mid-1990's.* BELOW: *The crystal clear waters off Tobermory, such as these at Cove Island, are easily explored in an inflatable boat.* PHOTOS BY CRIS KOHL.

SCOVILLE, PHILO --- The captain alone died when this 325-ton schooner, built at Cleveland, OH, in 1863, dragged her anchors and struck the north shore of

Russel Island on October 6, 1889. The wreckage lies on a slope in 35'-95' of water, with twin anchor chains running down that entire length.

SWEEPSTAKES --- See *The 100 Best Great Lakes Shipwrecks, Volume I*, pp. 219-221.

WALTERS, JOHN --- The 108' schooner, built at Kingston, ON, in 1852, was driven ashore and destroyed in the SW corner of Russel Island in 1896. This broken, scattered wreck, easily visible from the surface, lies in 6'-15'.

WETMORE, W.L. --- This 30-year-old steamer, launched at Cleveland, OH, was driven ashore during a storm on November 29, 1901, and pounded to pieces in the shallows. No lives were lost. One of her two towbarges, the JAMES C. KING, was also wrecked (see p. 476). The wreck lies broken, but with much to see and explore, in depths from 6'-20' off the NE corner of Russel Island. Her boiler, easily visible, rises to 6' of the surface.

Eriequest Marine Park
Leamington (Point Pelee), Ontario (Lake Erie)

Created in the mid-1990's, the boundaries of this underwater park include many of the shipwrecks off Point Pelee National Park and the town of Leamington, Ontario.

AMERICA --- This 240' sidewheel steamer, built at Port Huron, MI, in 1847, stranded off the NE tip of Pelee Island about 0.5 mile below the abandoned light-house on April 5, 1854. No lives were lost. The broken up remains lie in 15' of water. The boiler rises about 10'. LAT/LON: 41.49.679 / 82.38.069

ARMENIA --- The 288' schooner-barge, ARMENIA, loaded with ore, foundered in a storm on Wednesday, May 9, 1906, in Pigeon Bay, about 10 miles NW of Pelee Passage. The vessel, built in 1896 at West Bay City, MI, was dynamited to eliminate her as a threat to navigation. The remains lie broken and scattered in 35'-39' of water. LORAN: 43806.62 / 57091.06

BUTTERS, MARSHALL F. --- The 164' wooden lumber hooker, MARSHALL F. BUTTERS, was one of the four ships lost in the Black Friday Storm of October 20, 1916. No lives were lost when this vessel sank, unlike the tragic losses on the other three wrecks: MERIDA, JAMES B. COLGATE, and D.L. FILER. The BUTTERS, constructed at Milwaukee, WI, in 1882, lies in 62'-70' of water just within the Canadian side of the international boundary line. LORAN: 43791.13 / 57233.05, LAT/LON: 41.43.639 / 82.17.368

CASE -- This 286' steamer, loaded with coal (which was later salvaged), stranded, caught fire, and broke up in a storm about 600' off the NW side of East Sister Island, ON, on Tuesday, May 1, 1917. No lives were lost. Built at Cleveland, OH, in 1889, this wreck lies broken and scattered in about 20' of water. LORAN: 43742.28 / 56956.58, LAT/LON: 41.48.59 / 82.51.67

CLARION --- See *The 100 Best Great Lakes Shipwrecks, Volume I,* pp. 78-83.

CONEMAUGH --- The 251' wooden freighter, built in 1880 at Bay City, MI, stranded on the west side of Point Pelee's tip on Wednesday, November 21, 1906, and became a total loss, fortunately with no loss of life. The remains lie broken and scattered in 16'-20' of water, and can be reached from shore about 400' away. LORAN: 43835.72 / 57163.12

DOMINION --- This dredge, about 75' long, capsized while being towed and sank in 36'-40' of water about three miles east of Point Pelee on Friday, October 28, 1892. No lives were lost. LORAN: 43880.93 / 57218.21

DUNBAR, GEORGE --- This small steamer, measuring 133' in length and built in Alleghan, MI, in 1867, carried a cargo of coal when she sprang a leak and sank just on the Canadian side of the international boundary line off Point Pelee on Sunday, June 29, 1902. Her remains lie in 42'-45' of water. LORAN: 43729.63 / 57076.39, LAT/LON: 41.40.627 / 82.33.891

GOULD, JAY --- The 213' wooden freighter, built in 1869 at Buffalo, NY, sprang a leak and foundered about five miles SE of Point Pelee on June 17, 1918, with no lives lost. The wreck, dynamited as a menace to navigation, lies in 38'-44' of water, with its lay steeple compound engine, one of the first, rising higher. LORAN: 43829,24 / 57202.61, LAT/LON: 41.51.534 / 82.24.591

JORGE B. --- This diesel fish tug sank on September 16, 1983, about 3/4 of a mile east of Point Pelee. Half the crew swam to safety on shore, while the other three drowned. The wreck sits in 27'-33' of water. LORAN: 43851.23 / 57184.05

MAGNET --- Lying in about 33'-35' of water five miles SW of Colchester Reef, the 145', coal-laden, twin-masted schooner, built in 1856 in East Saginaw, MI, foundered in a storm with no lives lost on September 12, 1900. The wreck was dynamited as a navigation danger. LORAN: 43757.84 / 56926.72

MINCH, PHILLIP --- The most impressive feature of this wreck site in about 48' of water, the towering steeple compound steam engine, was accidentally knocked over by a passing ore ship in 1996 and now lies on its side. This 275' wooden steamer, built in 1888 at Cleveland, OH, caught on fire and sank with no loss of lives on November 20, 1904, just inside the Canadian line at the international border eight miles east of Middle Island. LORAN: 43741,93 / 57106.21, LAT/LON: 41.41.301 / 82.30.813

NORTHERN INDIANA --- Built in 1852 at Buffalo, NY, this 300' paddlewheel steamer burned and sank with great loss of life (about 28) on July 17, 1856 just west of Point Pelee's tip. The wreckage lies broken and scattered in 22'-25' of water. LORAN: 43830.71 / 57160.44, LAT/LON: 41.53.888 / 82.30.605

PACKARD, CHARLES B. --- This 180' wooden steamer sank in about 37'-40' of water after striking the sunken ship, ARMENIA (see p. 478) about seven miles west of Pelee Passage on September 16, 1906. No lives were lost. The machinery and propeller were removed before this vessel was dynamited. The boiler remains among debris on a silty bottom. LORAN: 43817.25 / 57073.72

SPECULAR --- A collision with the steamer, DENVER, sank the iron-ore-laden, 263' SPECULAR on Wednesday, August 22, 1900. Built in 1882 at Cleveland, OH, this ship's remains lie in 35'-38' of water. Engine, boiler, anchor, and propeller form the highlights of this site. LORAN: 43795.74 / 57128.33

STEWART, DAVID --- This 181' schooner, built at Cleveland, OH, in 1867, was blown ashore in a gale on the west side of Point Pelee on Friday, October 6, 1893, with no loss of life. The broken, scattered remains lie flat in about 21' of water. LORAN: 43858.03 / 57160.25

STONE, GEORGE --- Lying in 32'-45' of water on the south edge of Grubb's Reef to the SW of Point Pelee, this 270' wooden steamer, built in 1893 at West Bay City, MI, stranded and caught on fire on Wednesday, October 13, 1909. Six lives were lost. LORAN: 43820.03 / 57135.26

TASMANIA --- This four-masted, 221' schooner, built in 1871 at Port Huron, MI, had been reduced to a tow-barge when she foundered in a severe storm southwest of Point Pelee on Friday, October 20, 1905, with the loss of all hands (8). The remains lie scattered in 38'-40' of water. LORAN: 43786.98 / 57140.18

TIOGA --- This 177' steamer caught on fire and sank about five miles west of Point Pelee on October 5, 1877, with no lives lost. Built in 1862 at Cleveland, OH, the TIOGA sits in about 40' of water. Highlights include the capstan, windlass, rudder, boiler, and propeller. LORAN: 43813.75 / 57116.12

VANCE, DAVID --- This schooner (206' 6" x 33' 7" x 14' 4"), built at Buffalo, NY, in 1874, sank SW of Point Pelee after a collision with the steamer, LIZZIE A. LAW, on Thursday, July 20, 1893. All lives were dramatically saved. The wreck lies flattened in about 40' of water. LORAN: 43813.84 / 57144.29

WESEE --- This burning ship was purposely stranded on the NW side of Middle Sister Island on Monday, November 12, 1923. No lives were lost, and the 265' wooden steamer, built in 1901 at Green Bay, WI, broke up over time, with most of her remains lying scattered in 18'-22' of water. The engine and boilers were removed. LORAN: 43739.2 / 56895.55

WILCOX, M.I. --- This 137', three-masted schooner, built in 1866 at Toledo, OH, sprang a leak and sank in about 22' of water on Tuesday, May 8, 1906, with no lives lost. The broken and scattered wreckage includes a windlass, donkey boiler, capstan, anchor, wheel, deadeyes, and flattened rudder. This wreck was located on July 2, 1990, by Ed Fabok, Joe Drummond, and Lloyd and Betty Kerr. LORAN: 43802.26 / 56959.56

WILLIS --- See *The 100 Best Great Lakes Shipwrecks, Volume I,* pp. 126-128.

WORTHINGTON, GEORGE -- This twin-masted schooner (119' 9" x 25' 2" x 10' 1"), built in 1852 at Euclid Creek, OH, sank in about 40' of water after a collision with the schooner, GEORGE W. DAVIS, off Colchester Reef on July 12, 1887. No lives were lost. This intact, upright wreck sports twin bow anchors, windlass, deadeyes, centerboard, and tools on deck. The wreck was discovered on July 28, 1987, by Ed Fabok and Art Vermette. LORAN: 43800.0 / 56994.4

Isle Royale National Park, Michigan (Lake Superior)

Isle Royale National Park was created in 1940, not specifically as an underwater park, but the shipwrecks in the island's waters fall under National Park jurisdiction. It is illegal to remove anything from any shipwreck in the Great Lakes; from a National Park, it is even more illegal! Scuba divers must register at a ranger station before diving. Boats from Canada must clear customs.

Isle Royale, a U.S. National Park, provides wooden lean-tos on a first come, first served basis for visitors like Gary Gentile willing to rough it.   PHOTO BY CRIS KOHL.

ALGOMA --- This 262' steel passenger steamer, built in Scotland in 1883, stranded on Isle Royale on November 7, 1885, with the loss of 45 or 47 lives, Lake Superior's worst marine disaster. Wreckage lies in 15' to about 100' in three gullies, with some pieces in water to about 150'. LORAN: 31748.36 / 46187.83, LAT/LON: 48.06.46 / 88.31.54

AMERICA --- See *The 100 Best Great Lakes Shipwrecks, Volume II*, pp. 357-358.

CHISHOLM, HENRY --- This 256' wooden steamer struck the Rock of Ages Reef on October 21, 1898, broke up, and sank, fortunately with no loss of life. The vessel was built at Cleveland in 1880. This wreckage, which is intermingled with that of the CUMBERLAND, lies in 20'-90' of water. The CHISHOLM'S engine lies on the other side of the reef in 140' (see *The 100 Best Great Lakes Shipwrecks, Vol. I*, Appendix C: 100 Deep Great Lakes Shipwrecks,

p. 253). Main wreckage: LORAN: 31927.24 / 46066.70, LAT/LON: 47.52.73 / 89.18.33

CONGDON, CHESTER A. --- See *The 100 Best Great Lakes Shipwrecks, Volume II,* pp. 388-391, and *The 100 Best Great Lakes Shipwrecks, Vol. I,* Appendix C: 100 Deep Great Lakes Shipwrecks, pp. 253-254.

COX, GEORGE M. --- See *The 100 Best Great Lakes Shipwrecks, Volume II,* pp. 392-398.

CUMBERLAND --- The 205' sidewheel steamer, CUMBERLAND, was only six years old when the ship stranded on Rock of Ages Reef on July 26, 1877 and broke up with no loss of life. The ship had been built in 1871 at Port Robinson, Ontario. The scattered wreckage lies intermingled with that of the HENRY CHISHOLM in 20'-90' of water in a jumble of timbers and machinery such as engine, boilers, rudder, paddlewheel, and propeller. LORAN: 31927.24 / 46066.70, LAT/LON: 47.52.73 / 89.18.33

EMPEROR --- See *The 100 Best Great Lakes Shipwrecks, Volume II,* pp. 401-405, and *The 100 Best Great Lakes Shipwrecks, Vol. I,* Appendix C: 100 Deep Great Lakes Shipwrecks, p. 254.

GLENLYON --- This 328' steel freighter, launched in 1893 at Bay City, MI, as the WILLIAM H. GRATWICK, stranded on a reef off the south shore of Isle Royale on November 1, 1924 , with wheat. No lives were lost in this mishap. The broken-up wreckage lies in 10'-50' of water, with parts of the stern cabin in 100'. LORAN: 31808.65 / 46188.57, LAT/LON: 47.57.21 / 88.45.01

KAMLOOPS --- See *The 100 Best Great Lakes Shipwrecks, Vol. I,* Appendix C: 100 Deep Great Lakes Shipwrecks, pp. 255-256.

MONARCH --- See *The 100 Best Great Lakes Shipwrecks, Vol. I,* Appendix C: 100 Deep Great Lakes Shipwrecks, p. 258.

Apostle Islands National Lakeshore, Bayfield, Wisconsin (Lake Superior)

Wisconsin's Apostle Islands National Lakeshore, created in 1970, includes 21 of the 22 Apostle Islands and has jurisdiction over water that is within one-quarter mile of any shoreline. Although this entity was not specifically created as an underwater park or preserve, scuba divers must procure a free permit, available from ranger stations or the Visitor Centers at Bayfield and Little Sand Bay, before they can explore the shipwrecks in these waters.

COFFINBERRY, H.D. --- This 191' wooden steamer, built in 1874 at East Saginaw, MI, was abandoned at Red Cliff Bay in 1913 after serving many years in the iron ore and lumber trades. Portions of the wreck are above water, while the rest sits in 6'. LORAN: 32395.65 / 46144.68, LAT/LON: 46.52.84 / 90.46.26

FEDORA --- This 282' wooden steamer, built in 1889 at West Bay City, MI, burned to a total loss from an exploding lantern at Red Cliff on September 20, 1901. The captain grounded her in the shallows before all on board abandoned ship. The remains, partially exposed, sit in 10' of water. LORAN: 32403.33 / 46153.52, LAT/LON: 46.51.586 / 90.46.707

LUCERNE --- The three-masted, 195' schooner, LUCERNE, foundered in a severe storm with all hands (10) and a load of iron ore on November 17, 1886, in 24' of water NE of Long Island. The bow of this surprisingly intact shipwreck rises 9' off the bottom. LORAN: 32434.64 / 46234.92, LAT/LON: 46.43.39 / 90.45.03

McCOOL, FIN --- Quite intact, this 135' barge, built in 1926 at Ashland, WI, sank in 20' of water in Bayfield harbor in 1964. It is easily accessible from shore, but the harbor sees much boating traffic. LORAN: 32423.31 / 46171.58

NOQUE BAY --- This 205' schooner-barge, built in 1872 at Trenton, MI, burned to a complete loss in 12' of water in Julian Bay on the SE side of Stockton Island on October 6, 1905 with no loss of life. LORAN: 32351.36 / 46184.61, LAT/LON: 46.55.563 / 90.32.712

OTTAWA --- This large, powerful, 151' tugboat lies about 70' from the H.D. COFFINBERRY, in about 25' of water. Built at Chicago in 1881, the OTTAWA burned to a complete loss with no lives lost on November 29, 1909, at Red Cliff Bay. LORAN: 32395.59 / 46144.62, LAT/LON: 46.52.85 / 90.46.25

PRETORIA --- This enormous, 338', three-masted schooner, built at West Bay City, MI, in 1900, sank in the gale of September 2, 1905, which also sank the steamer, SEVONA (see pp. 450-452). Five of the 11 people on board perished. This wreck lies in 55' of water about one mile off the NE shore of Outer Island, about 30 miles from Bayfield, WI. LORAN: 32288.02 / 46141.14, LAT/LON: 47.05.35 / 90.23.64

SEVONA --- See *The 100 Best Great Lakes Shipwrecks, Volume II*, pp. 450-452.

Michigan's Underwater Preserves System

Michigan's underwater preserve system, created through legislation supported by Michigan sport divers, began with the establishment in 1980 of a few areas known for their high concentrations of shipwrecks, and has since grown to nine in number, with two more proposed preserves. To quote from the *Dive Michigan Underwater Preserves* brochure, "...It is a felony to remove or disturb artifacts in the Great Lakes. Those caught removing portholes, anchors, anchor chain, or other 'souvenirs' will have their boats, cars, and equipment confiscated and will face up to two years' imprisonment and stiff fines...." The Michigan Department of Natural Resources has set up a hotline number to report artifact thefts from shipwrecks: 1-800-292-7800. One popular slogan is, "Come to enjoy, not to destroy." Our shipwrecks are limited in numbers, and they are non-renewable.

Alger Underwater Preserve, Munising, Michigan (Lake Superior)

BERMUDA --- See *The 100 Best Great Lakes Shipwrecks, Volume II,* pp. 373-377.

GEORGE --- The 203' schooner, built in 1873 at Manitowoc, WI, stranded and sank off Pictured Rocks about two miles east of Miner's Castle on October 25, 1893 with a load of coal and no loss of life. The remains lie in 15' of water. LORAN: 31604.48 / 47430.63

HETTLER, HERMAN H. --- This 210' wooden steamer, built in 1890 at West Bay City, MI, stranded in a storm on November 23, 1926, near Munising, MI. The crew escaped unharmed. Although dynamited as an obstruction, this wreck's huge pieces are fascinating to explore in 20'-36' of water. LORAN: 31632.18 / 47431.39, LAT/LON: 46.29.03 / 86.35.98

KIOWA --- See *The 100 Best Great Lakes Shipwrecks, Volume II,* pp. 408-410.

MANHATTAN --- Burned after stranding off the south end of Grand Island with a cargo of wheat on October 26, 1903, this 252' wooden steamer, built in 1887 at Wyandotte, MI, lies in 20'-32' of water. LORAN: 31648.40 / 47438.13, LAT/LON: 46.28.02 / 86.36.56

MOORE, SMITH --- See *The 100 Best Great Lakes Shipwrecks, Volume II,* pp. 422-426.

SELVICK, STEVEN M. --- See *The 100 Best Great Lakes Shipwrecks, Volume II,* pp. 447-449.

SITKA --- Not far away from the KIOWA shipwreck off Au Sable Point, MI, (see pp. 408-410), lies the 272' wooden steamer, SITKA. Built in 1887 at West Bay City, MI, this ship stranded and broke up on October 4, 1904 with no lives lost. The remains are in 15'-25' of water. LORAN: 31474.03 / 47421.12

SUPERIOR --- A tragic loss of 35 lives resulted from the 184' passenger sidewheeler, built in 1845 at Perrysburg, OH, stranding just west of Spray Falls at Pictured Rocks on October 30, 1856. The boilers, visible from the surface, and wooden hull sections lie in 6'-33' of water. LAT/LON: 46.33.45 / 86.24.91

The incredible scenic beauty of Pictured Rocks National Seashore skirts the Alger Underwater Preserve near Munising, MI. PHOTO BY CRIS KOHL.

DeTour Underwater Preserve (proposed), DeTour, Michigan (Lake Huron)

AGNES W. --- This 264' wooden steamer, built at Milwaukee in 1887, stranded and broke up on Traverse Point south of Drummond Island during a storm on July 2, 1918. The machinery was removed from this wreck, which sits in 2'-12' of water. LORAN: 30869.81/48191.38, LAT/LON: 45.55.47 / 83.42.48

CULLEN, JOHN W. --- Built in 1883 at Milwaukee, WI, and abandoned in 1933, the remains of this 141' schooner lie in 6'-41' of water between DeTour Village and Frying Pan Island. It is only about 300' east of the SAINTE MARIE wreck. LORAN: 30922.21 / 48136.75, LAT/LON: 45.59.32 / 83.53.67

FORD, J.C. --- A fire and explosion on November 26, 1924, NE of DeTour off Little Trout Island, destroyed this 172' lumber steamer, built at Grand Haven, MI, in 1889. Visible from the surface, this wreck sits in 5'-15' of water. LORAN: 30894.77 / 48116.91, LAT/LON: 46.02.63 / 83.50.21

GENERAL --- This 97' tug, built in 1899 at West Bay City, MI, burned and sank at the NW end of Frying Pan Island on April 7, 1930. The engine and machinery were salvaged from the 15'-21' depths. LORAN: 30923.48 / 48137.05, LAT/LON: 45.59.24 / 83.53.88

MERRILL, JOHN B. --- See *The 100 Best Great Lakes Shipwrecks, Volume I,* pp. 179-180.

ROME --- This 265' wooden steamer lies in about 16' of water accessible from shore at the NW end of Lime Island at the harbor entrance in the St. Mary's River. Built in 1879 at Cleveland, OH, the ROME burned to a complete loss on November 17, 1909 with no lives lost. LORAN: 30946.35 / 48073.10, LAT/LON: 46.05.24 / 84.00.77

SAINTE MARIE --- This 288' railroad car ferry, built in 1893 at Wyandotte, MI, and used in the Straits of Mackinac, was abandoned in the mid-1920's near DeTour. It sits in depths to 40', with part of the wreck visible above water. LORAN: 30922.26 / 48136.71, LAT/LON: 45.59.33 / 83.53.67

SUPERIOR --- Built in 1881 at Fort Howard, WI, as the sloop, Mentor, this 138' wooden scow steamer burned to a total loss at DeTour Harbor entrance on June 11, 1929. Only large timbers remain in 8'-14' depths. LORAN: 30922.88 / 48133.28

TWO MYRTLES --- This 78' steamer, used as a lighthouse tender, was built in 1889 at Manitowoc, WI, and abandoned in the 1930's in 8'-14' about 300' north of the east-west DeTour Harbor breakwall. LORAN: 30922.48 / 48131.64, LAT/LON: 45.59.83 / 83.53.96

Keweenaw Underwater Preserve, Keweenaw Peninsula, Michigan (Lake Superior)

ASTOR, JOHN JACOB --- The remains of this 78' brig, which stranded here on Sept. 21, 1844, lie in 10'-14' of water just west of the Copper Harbor Lighthouse dock. This, the first commercial ship on this lake, was built in 1835.

COLORADO --- This 254' wooden steamer stranded in a storm on September 19, 1898. The remains lie in 22'-36' of water on Sawtooth Reef near Eagle River, MI. LORAN: 31825.07 / 46553.24, LAT/LON: 47.25.46 / 88.18.02

FERN --- This 65' tug was salvaging metal from the COLORADO when a storm destroyed it and the entire crew on June 29, 1901. This wreck lies scattered with the other wreck in 15'-22' of water on Sawtooth Reef near Eagle River, MI. LORAN: 31825.12 / 46553.18, LAT/LON: 47.25.46 / 88.18.02

GAZELLE --- This 158' sidewheel steamer, built in 1858 at Newport (now Marine City), MI, stranded in a storm while entering Eagle Harbor, MI, on September 8, 1860. The remains lie in 10'-20' of water. LAT/LON: 47.27.43 / 88.09.27

LANGHAM --- See *The 100 Best Great Lakes Shipwrecks, Volume II,* pp. 411-414.

MESQUITE --- See *The 100 Best Great Lakes Shipwrecks, Volume II,* pp. 418-421.

MORELAND, WILLIAM C. --- This new, 580' steel steamer stranded with a load of iron ore on Sawtooth Reef because of dense smoke from a forest fire on October 18, 1910. The stern half was salvaged, but the rest sits in 20'-36' of water. LORAN: 31833.22 / 46551.01, LAT/LON: 47.24.84 / 88.19.73

PICKANDS, JAMES --- See *The 100 Best Great Lakes Shipwrecks, Volume II*, pp. 438-439.

SCOTIA --- A storm stranded this 231' iron steamer off Keweenaw Point on October 24, 1884. The remains sit flat in 15'. LAT/LON: 47.25.86 / 87.42.28

ST. JOSEPH, CITY OF/ TRANSPORT --- Both of these old, 254' ships (one of steel, the other of iron) were used as barges when they stranded in a storm on Sept. 21, 1942. These wrecks lie in 10'-35' of water, the TRANSPORT closer to shore. LORAN: 31777.77 / 46581.52, LAT/LON: 47.28.12 / 88.06.68

SUPERIOR, CITY OF --- This 190' wooden steamer stranded on November 11, 1857, three months after being launched. The remains lie in front of the Copper Harbor Lighthouse in 10'-14' of water. LAT/LON: 47.28.40 / 87.51.72

TIOGA --- See *The 100 Best Great Lakes Shipwrecks, Volume II*, pp. 455-456.

TRAVELLER --- This 179' sidewheeler burned in Eagle Harbor on August 17, 1865. The wreck lies in shifting sands in 15'-22'. LAT/LON: 47.27.62 / 88.09.11

WASAGA --- This 238' wooden steamer burned in Copper Harbor on November 7, 1910. This wreck lies in 25'-36' of water. LAT/LON: 47.28.22 / 87.52.93

Manitou Passages Underwater Preserve, Michigan (Lake Michigan)

BRADLEY, ALVA --- See *The 100 Best Great Lakes Shipwrecks, Volume II*, pp. 271-274.

CONGRESS --- See *The 100 Best Great Lakes Shipwrecks, Vol. I*, Appendix C: 100 Deep Great Lakes Shipwrecks, pp. 249-250.

CROUSE, J.S. --- This 90', 21-year-old, wooden steamer burned in Glen Haven, MI, harbor on November 15, 1919, and sits in 10'-20' of water. LORAN: 31840.74 / 48401.71, LAT/LON: 44.55.32 / 86.01.30

FLYING CLOUD --- This 133' schooner, built in 1854, stranded and broke up near Glen Arbor, MI, in Oct., 1892. No lives were lost. The wreck lies broken in 15'. LORAN: 31816.47 / 48403.46, LAT/LON: 44.56.18 / 85.57.40

FROST, WALTER L. --- This 235' wooden steamer lies broken in 10'-15' of water 600' S of the MORAZAN, on S. Manitou Island. The FROST stranded there on Nov. 4, 1903. LORAN: 31859.14 / 48339.44, LAT/LON: 44.59.67 / 86.08.69

GRAVES, WILLIAM T. --- This large, wooden steamer stranded on North Manitou Shoal on October 31, 1885, and now lies broken in 10' of water. LORAN: 31802.78 / 48330.72, LAT/LON: 45.02.96 / 86.00.43

MCBRIDE, JAMES --- This 121' brig, stranded in a storm at Sleeping Bear Bay on October 19, 1857, lies in shifting sands in 5'-15' of water. LORAN: 31864.88 / 48408.67, LAT/LON: 45.02.34 / 86.00.02

MONTAUK --- In 35' of water, this 137' schooner stranded on N. Manitou I. on Nov. 23, 1882. LORAN: 31759.55 / 48270.60, LAT/LON: 45.09.54 / 85.59.45

MOORE, H.D. --- In 10'-12' of water on the north side of Gull Point, S. Manitou Island, lie the remains of this 103' schooner which stranded here on Sept. 10, 1907. LORAN: 27999.71 / 48514.18, LAT/LON: 45.02.02 / 86.04.44

MORAZAN, FRANCISCO --- See *The 100 Best Great Lakes Shipwrecks, Volume II*, pp. 314-316.

NEWLAND, J.B. --- In 4'-10' of water on North Manitou Shoal lies this 112' schooner which stranded here on Sept. 8, 1910. LORAN: 31803.33 / 48338.15

RALPH, P.J. --- This 211' wooden steamer leaked and sank near South Manitou Harbor on September 8, 1924, with no lives lost. Wreckage lies in 10'-45' along a dropoff. LORAN: 31839.51 / 48333.51, LAT/LON: 45.01.09 / 86.06.02

RISING SUN --- This 133' wooden steamer stranded in 6'-12' of water just north of Pyramid Point, MI, on October 29, 1917, and broke up in place. No lives were lost. LORAN: 31799.62 / 48386.79, LAT/LON: 44.58.22 / 85.55.95

SUPPLY --- In 8'-10' of water lies this 132' brig, built in 1855 at Buffalo, NY. The ship stranded on North Manitou Island in November, 1869, with a brick cargo. LORAN: 31769.80 / 48285.05, LAT/LON: 44.58.20 / 85.58.51

TAYLOR, GENERAL --- This 173' wooden steamer, built in 1848, stranded on Sleeping Bear Pt. on Oct. 3, 1862. It lies in 10'. LAT/LON: 44.53.67 / 86.04.54

THREE BROTHERS --- See *The 100 Best Great Lakes Shipwrecks, Volume II*, pp. 337-339.

Marquette Underwater Preserve, Marquette, Michigan (Lake Superior)

ARCTIC --- This 237' sidewheel steamer sank in 5'-105' of water at Huron Island in fog on May 28, 1860. LAT/LON: 46.57.76 / 87.59.86

DESOTO --- In 8'-10' of water in Marquette Harbor lies this wooden bark which stranded in a gale on December 4, 1869. LAT/LON: 46.32.10 / 87.23.55

FLORIDA --- This 299-ton schooner lies close to the DESOTO in 6'-8' of water, having stranded there on November 17, 1886. LAT/LON: 46.32.10 / 87.23.55

KERSHAW, CHARLES J. --- This 223' wooden steamer grounded two miles south of Marquette, MI, on September 29, 1895, with no lives lost. The wreck lies scattered in 25' of water. LAT/LON: 46.39.56 / 87.21.80

LEUTY, D. --- About 800' off Marquette's Lighthouse Point, in 30'-40' of water, lie the remains of this 179' wooden steamer, which stranded there during a blinding blizzard on October 31, 1911. LAT/LON: 46.32.77 / 87.22.44

MARION L./SUPERIOR --- Both of these abandoned fish tugs lie in about 20' of water in busy Marquette Lower Harbor. LAT/LON: 46.32.46 / 87.23.33

NESTOR, GEORGE --- Just off Huron Island's lighthouse, in 20' to over 100' of water, lie the remains of this 207' schooner-barge which stranded here in a storm on April 30, 1909, with seven lives lost. LAT/LON: 46.58.01 / 88.00.23

QUEEN CITY --- In 10'-15' off Chocolay Beach lie the remains of this 365-ton schooner, stranded there in Nov., 1864. LAT/LON: 46.29.39 / 87.18.65

SHEADLE, J.H. --- Only the rudder and one propeller blade, plus jettisoned iron ore cargo, remain here in 15' where this 550' steel ship stranded for a month in late 1920. The ship was scrapped in 1980. LAT/LON: 46.34.10 / 87.23.20

SHERMAN, GEORGE --- This 140' schooner stranded at Shot Point east of Marquette on October 23, 1887, and lies in 10'-12'. LAT/LON: 46.29.88 /87.09.65

SOUTHWEST --- See *The 100 Best Great Lakes Shipwrecks, Volume II,* pp. 453-454.

Sanilac Shores Underwater Preserve, Port Sanilac, Michigan (Lake Huron)

BREDEN, JOHN --- This three-masted, 130' schooner foundered on July 21, 1899, with the loss of three lives about 5.5 miles SE of Lexington, MI, lying in 50' of water. LORAN: 30823.42 / 49595.72, LAT/LON: 43.12.26 / 82.26.32

CHECOTAH --- This 199' schooner-barge foundered in a storm on October 30, 1906 about 12 miles NNE of Port Sanilac, MI, and lies in 92'-116' of water. LORAN: 30761.33 / 49413.52, LAT/LON: 43.36.08 / 82.28.17

GARDNER, F.B. --- On September 15, 1904, this 139' schooner burned and sank in 48'-55' of water six miles NE of Port Sanilac, MI. The wreck was dynamited. LORAN: 30802.42 / 49407.21, LAT/LON: 43.31.62 / 82.31.77

GENOA, CITY OF --- This 301' wooden steamer sank in a collision in the St. Clair River on August 26, 1911, and was finally scuttled in Lake Huron in 53'-65' in 1915. LORAN: 30805.12 / 49624.95, LAT/LON: 43.08.79 / 82.22.31

MARY ALICE B. --- See *The 100 Best Great Lakes Shipwrecks, Volume I,* pp. 174-178.

NEW YORK --- See *The 100 Best Great Lakes Shipwrecks, Volume I,* pp. 184-186.

NORTH STAR --- See *The 100 Best Great Lakes Shipwrecks, Volume I*, pp. 190-193.

PRICE, CHARLES S. --- See *The 100 Best Great Lakes Shipwrecks, Volume I*, pp. 200-206.

QUEEN CITY --- Stranded nine miles SE of Lexington, MI, on August 17, 1863, this 292' paddlewheel steamer broke up and sank in 44'-52' of water. No lives were lost. LORAN: 30831.22 / 49622.35, LAT/LON: 43.09.18 / 82.25.77

REGINA --- See *The 100 Best Great Lakes Shipwrecks, Volume I*, pp. 207-212.

SPORT --- See *The 100 Best Great Lakes Shipwrecks, Volume I*, pp. 213-218.

STREET, CHARLES A. --- Broken up in 5'-15' of water about 12 miles north of Port Sanilac, this 165' wooden steamer burned and was grounded on July 20, 1908. LORAN: 30818.23 / 49413.12, LAT/LON: 43.35.50 / 82.27.51

STRONG, ELIZA H. --- This 205' wooden steamer burned about one mile off Lexington, MI, and sank in 25'-32' of water on October 26, 1904. LORAN: 30847.03 / 49570.42, LAT/LON: 43.15.71 / 82.30.58

WILLIAMS, COLONEL A.B. --- This 110' schooner, upright and intact in 75'-85' of water, foundered in a storm in 1864 about 12 miles NE of Port Sanilac, MI. LORAN: 30779.12 / 49407.24, LAT/LON: 43.36.47 / 82.30.67

Southwest Michigan Underwater Preserve (proposed),
Muskegon to New Buffalo, Michigan (Lake Michigan)

FRANCIE --- This sailing dredge converted to a pleasure craft was purposely scuttled by scuba divers for the creation of a dive site two miles west of Saugatuck harbor in 88' to 104' of water. LORAN: 32644.68 / 49724.14.

GREEN BAY, CITY OF --- This 145' schooner stranded in the same storm which claimed the HAVANA on Oct. 3, 1887, with 6 out of 7 lives lost. This scattered wreck lies in 5'-15' about 2.5 miles S of the South Haven piers, 550' from shore. LORAN: 32773.41 / 49926.64, LAT/LON: 42.22.00 / 86.17. 98

HAVANA --- Sitting in 48'-53' of water a mile offshore and six miles north of St. Joseph, MI, this 135' schooner foundered on October 3, 1887, with three lives lost. LORAN: 32888.11 / 50024.94, LAT/LON: 42.11.71 / 86.25.74

IRONSIDES --- See *The 100 Best Great Lakes Shipwrecks, Volume II*, pp. 300-301.

ROCKAWAY --- This 106' scow-schooner foundered in 63'-70' of water 2.5 miles NW of South Haven, MI, on November 19, 1891, with no lives lost. Many of the artifacts were removed by archaeologists and are on exhibit in the Michigan Maritime Museum at South Haven, MI. LORAN: 42264.44 / 86184.52, LAT/LON: 42.26.37 / 86.18.49

VERANO --- See *The 100 Best Great Lakes Shipwrecks, Volume II*, pp. 340-342.

Straits of Mackinac Underwater Preserve, Mackinac, Michigan (Lakes Michigan and Huron)

ALBEMARLE --- This new, 154' schooner stranded on November 6, 1867. The wreck lies broken up in 10'-13' of water, nine miles SE of Old Mackinac Point, north of Point Nipigon, and 300' NW of the HENRY CLAY wreck. LORAN: 31188.72 / 48183.14, LAT/LON: 45.42.57 / 84.33.51

ANGLO-SAXON/J.A. SMITH --- The wreckage of two ships are mingled at this site. The ANGLO-SAXON, a 134' schooner, and the J.A. SMITH, a 138' schooner, stranded together just off shore 12 miles west of Old Mackinac Point on September 8, 1887 and became total losses. The broken, scattered remains, reachable from shore, lie in 10'-13' of water. LORAN: 31309.63 / 48102.82, LAT/LON: 45.45.42 / 84.57.25

BARNUM, WILLIAM H. --- See *The 100 Best Great Lakes Shipwrecks, Volume I*, pp. 143-144.

CANISTEO --- This 196' steamer, built in 1862 at Buffalo, NY, stranded half a mile east of Waugoshance Light on October 14, 1880. She lies broken up in 15' of water. LORAN: 31341.92 / 48070.78, LAT/LON: 45.47.32 / 85.04.75

CEDARVILLE --- See *The 100 Best Great Lakes Shipwrecks, Volume I*, pp. 145-148.

CLAY, HENRY --- This 87' brig stranded off Point Nipigon on December 3, 1850. The wreck lies broken up in 10'-13' of water near the ALBEMARLE wreck. LORAN: 31189.73 / 48183.74, LAT/LON: 45.43.33 / 84.32.31

Diver Joan Forsberg explores the schooner, NORTHWEST'S, *donkey boiler. More than a dozen wrecks in the Straits are popular with visiting divers.*   PHOTO BY CRIS KOHL.

JOHNSON, C.H. --- This 137' schooner stranded and broke up on St. Helena Island about 10 miles west of St. Ignace, MI, in late September, 1895. She lies in 10'-15'. LORAN: 31247.14 / 48061.78, LAT/LON: 45.52.20 / 84.50.08

MAITLAND --- See *The 100 Best Great Lakes Shipwrecks, Volume II*, pp. 304-306.

MCBRIER, FRED --- This 161' wooden steamer sank after a collision with the steamer, PROGRESS, on October 3, 1890. No lives were lost. The wreck sits upright and intact in 92'-105' of often silty water, nine miles west of Old Mackinac Point. LORAN: 31287.82 / 48085.33, LAT/LON: 45.48.11 / 84.55.09

MINNEAPOLIS --- This wreck sits in 125' just SW of the Mackinac Bridge, but her smokestack rises to 75'. This 226' wooden steamer was sunk by ice on April 4, 1894, with no lives lost. Beware of current and silt. LORAN: 31226.21 / 48111.21, LAT/LON: 45.48.32 / 84.43.54

NORTHWEST --- Six miles west of Old Mackinac Point, in 75' of water, lie the remains of this 223', four-masted schooner which sank on April 6, 1898, when ice punctured her hull. Chuck and Jeri Feltner found this wreck in 1978. LORAN: 31270.31 / 48102.29, LAT/LON: 45.47.32 / 84.51.30

OUTHWAITE, J.H. ---In 30' of water 10 miles ESE of Old Mackinac Point lies the wreck of this 224' wooden steamer which stranded on November 28, 1905, no lives lost. LORAN: 31187.37 / 48184.37, LAT/LON: 45.42.28 / 84.33.18

SANDUSKY --- See *The 100 Best Great Lakes Shipwrecks, Volume II*, pp. 326-331.

ST. ANDREW --- This 135' schooner sank after a collision with the Peshtigo on June 26, 1878. The wreck lies in 54'-61' of water 11 miles SE of Old Mackinac Point. LORAN: 31180.39 / 48195.18, LAT/LON: 45.42.07 / 84.31.46

STALKER, M. --- Sitting upright and intact in 85' of water, this 135' schooner sank after a collision with the MUSKOKA on November 5, 1886, two miles east of Mackinac. LORAN: 31213.67 / 48125.98, LAT/LON: 45.47.38 / 84.41.04

WARD, EBER --- See *The 100 Best Great Lakes Shipwrecks, Vol. I*, Appendix C: 100 Deep Great Lakes Shipwrecks, pp. 252-253.

Thumb Area Underwater Preserve, Port Austin to Harbor Beach, Michigan (Lake Huron)

ALBANY --- See *The 100 Best Great Lakes Shipwrecks, Vol. I*, Appendix C (Deep Wrecks), p. 242.

BERLIN --- This 111' schooner, carrying a cargo of lumber and limestone, broke up off Pointe aux Barques, MI, on November 8, 1877 with the loss of four lives. She sits in 10' of water. LORAN: 30869.2 / 49170.7

BERTSCHY, JACOB --- This 139' steamer, in 10', stranded off Port Austin, MI, on Sept. 3, 1879. LORAN: 30861.7 / 49181.4, LAT/LON: 44.03.42 / 82.53.13

CHICKAMAUGA --- This 322' schooner-barge foundered on Sept. 12, 1919. The wreck was raised and removed in 1920 to half a mile E of Harbor Beach, MI, to 35' of water. LORAN: 30785.1 / 49292.7, LAT/LON: 43.50.83 / 82.37.39

DUNDERBERG --- See *The 100 Best Great Lakes Shipwrecks, Vol. I*, Appendix C: 100 Deep Great Lakes Shipwrecks, p. 243.

DORR, E.P. --- See *The 100 Best Great Lakes Shipwrecks, Vol. I*, Appendix C: 100 Deep Great Lakes Shipwrecks, p. 243.

GLENORCHY --- This 365' steel steamer sank in a collision in fog on October 29, 1924, about ten miles ESE of Harbor Beach, MI, in 102'-121' of water, no lives lost. LORAN: 30750.4 / 49314.2, LAT/LON: 43.48.39 / 82.31.68

GOLIATH --- Also referred to as *Goliah,* this early propeller-driven steamer exploded and sank on September 13, 1848 with the loss of 18 lives. The 131' vessel sits in 104' of water off Harbor Beach, MI. The wreck was discovered by David Trotter and his team in 1985. LORAN: 30761.8 / 49326.3

IRON CHIEF --- See *The 100 Best Great Lakes Shipwrecks, Vol. I*, Appendix C: 100 Deep Great Lakes Shipwrecks, p. 245.

MARQUIS --- Sitting in 10' of water, this 130' schooner stranded and broke up near Harbor Beach, MI, on November 12, 1892. LORAN: 30795.0 / 49266.4

MORRELL, DANIEL J. --- See *The 100 Best Great Lakes Shipwrecks, Vol. I*, Appendix C: 100 Deep Great Lakes Shipwrecks, pp. 245-247.

PHILADELPHIA --- See *The 100 Best Great Lakes Shipwrecks, Volume I*, pp. 196-199.

SMITH, GOVERNOR --- See *The 100 Best Great Lakes Shipwrecks, Vol. I*, Appendix C: 100 Deep Great Lakes Shipwrecks, p. 248.

Thunder Bay Underwater Preserve, Alpena, Michigan

ALLEN, E.B. --- This 111' schooner sank after a collision with the bark, NEWSBOY, on November 18, 1871, with no lives lost, and lies upright and intact 2.5 miles SE of the south end of Thunder Bay Island, in 92'-106' of water. LORAN: 30811.6 / 48693.0, LAT/LON: 45.00.92 / 83.09.78

BARGE NO. 1 --- In 39'-48', seven miles SE of Thunder Bay Harbor, sits this 309' barge which foundered on November 8, 1918. LORAN: 50865.0 / 48680.8

BIRCKHEAD, H.P. ---A mile south of the breakwall at the mouth of Thunder Bay River, this wreck lies in 10'-15' of water. This 156' steamer burned on September 30, 1905. LORAN: 30908.2 / 48651.4, LAT/LON: 45.03.03 / 83.25.81

FLINT, OSCAR T. --- This 218' wooden steamer burned to a total loss on November 25, 1909, with no lives lost. The wreck lies a mile offshore and four miles SE of Thunder Bay River, in 28'-36' of water. LORAN: 30879.8 / 48671.9, LAT/LON: 45.01.51 / 83.20.65

GARDNER, NELLIE --- See HORNER, MOLLY T.

GRECIAN --- See *The 100 Best Great Lakes Shipwrecks, Volume I,* pp. 156-157.

HANNA, D.R. --- This 532' steel freighter sank after a collision with the QUINCY A. SHAW on May 16, 1919. The wreck lies upside-down in 135' of water, but rises to about the 95' depth, 6.5 miles ESE of Thunder Bay Island Lighthouse. LORAN: 30771.3 / 48666.4, LAT/LON: 45.05.02 / 83.05.23

HORNER, MOLLY T. --- Also called the MOLLY H., this wreck could also be the NELLIE GARDNER. This wooden wreck is located in 15'-20' of water just north of South Point near the southern boundary of the underwater preserve between Scarecrow and Bird Islands. Nebulous histories. LORAN: 30893.7 / 48737.9

MONOHANSETT --- This 165' wooden steamer, built in 1872 at Gibraltar, MI, burned to a total loss on November 23, 1907, with no lives lost. The wreck lies about 600' SW of the old dock on the SW part of Thunder Bay Island, in 14'-20' of water. LORAN: 30822.5 / 48681.4, LAT/LON: 45.01.95 / 83.11.77

MONTANA --- See *The 100 Best Great Lakes Shipwrecks, Volume I,* pp. 181-183.

MONROVIA --- See *The 100 Best Great Lakes Shipwrecks, Vol. I,* Appendix C: 100 Deep Great Lakes Shipwrecks, p. 245.

NEW ORLEANS --- See *The 100 Best Great Lakes Shipwrecks, Vol. I,* Appendix C: 100 Deep Great Lakes Shipwrecks, p. 247.

NORDMEER --- See *The 100 Best Great Lakes Shipwrecks, Volume I,* pp. 187-189.

PEWABIC --- See *The 100 Best Great Lakes Shipwrecks, Vol. I,* Appendix C: 100 Deep Great Lakes Shipwrecks, p. 248.

PORTSMOUTH --- This 176' wooden steamer, built at Buffalo, NY, in 1852, stranded in a storm, then caught on fire and was destroyed on November 10, 1867. This wreck lies scattered off Middle Island in 15'. LORAN: 30847.6 / 48588.2

REND, WILLIAM P. --- This 287' barge (former steamer, launched in 1888 at West Bay City, MI) stranded on September 22, 1917, with no loss of life. The wreck lies in 15'-22' of water almost a mile east of the Huron Portland Cement Plant. LORAN: 30891.0 / 48649.5, LAT/LON: 45.03.72 / 83.23.38

THEW, W.P. --- A collision with the steamer, WILLIAM LIVINGSTON, sank the 132' wooden steamer, W.P. THEW, on June 22, 1909., with no loss of life. This small wreck lies two miles east of the Thunder Bay Island Lighthouse in 76'-86' of water. LORAN: 30802.7 / 48679.6, LAT/LON: 45.02.66 / 83.09.02

VAN VALKENBURG, LUCINDA --- This 128' schooner, built in 1862 at Tonawanda, NY, was run down by the steamer, LEHIGH, on June 1, 1887, with no lives lost. The wreck lies in 65'-72' of water, two miles NE of Thunder Bay Island. LORAN: 30807.3 / 48672.9, LAT/LON: 45.03.31 / 83.10.00

Whitefish Point Underwater Preserve, Whitefish Point, Michigan (Lake Superior)

COMET --- See *The 100 Best Great Lakes Shipwrecks, Vol. I*, Appendix C: 100 Deep Great Lakes Shipwrecks, p. 253.

COWLE, JOHN B. --- See *The 100 Best Great Lakes Shipwrecks, Vol. I*, Appendix C: 100 Deep Great Lakes Shipwrecks, p. 254.

DRAKE, M.M. --- This 201' wooden steamer attempted to remove the crew of its sinking barge, the 213' MICHIGAN, when heavy seas crashed the wooden ships together on October 2, 1901. Both vessels sank, with the loss of the MICHIGAN'S cook. The DRAKE lies about half a mile north of Vermilion Point, MI, in 42'-50' of water. The MICHIGAN has not yet been located. LORAN: 31167.5 / 47569.3, LAT/LON: 46.46.75 / 85.05.87

EUREKA --- This 138' schooner-barge foundered with all hands (6) and iron ore on Oct. 20, 1886, 6 miles N of Vermilion Point, MI. The broken remains lie in 48'-54' of water. LORAN: 31181.2 / 47524.4, LAT/LON: 46.50.15 / 85.10.76

INDIANA --- This 146' wooden steamer, launched in 1848 at Vermilion, OH, foundered 3.6 miles north of Crisp Point, MI, on June 6, 1858, with no loss of life. Found by John Steele (with Bill Cohrs and Kent Bellrichard) in 1972, this wreck's engine and boiler were removed by the Smithsonian Institute in Washington, D.C., for display purposes. What remains lies in 103'-118'. LORAN: 31215.1 / 47520.3, LAT/LON: 46.48.66 / 85.17.16

The Great Lakes Shipwreck Museum, housed in the restored Coast Guard and Lighthouse buildings at Whitefish Point, is the only museum in the Great Lakes devoted exclusively to shipwrecks. Go there between dives!   PHOTO BY CRIS KOHL.

MATHER, SAMUEL --- See *The 100 Best Great Lakes Shipwrecks, Vol. I*, Appendix C: 100 Deep Great Lakes Shipwrecks, p. 257.

MITCHELL, JOHN --- See *The 100 Best Great Lakes Shipwrecks, Vol. I*, Appendix C: 100 Deep Great Lakes Shipwrecks, p. 257.

MIZTEC --- This 194' schooner-barge foundered in a spring storm on May 15, 1921, with the loss of all hands (7), near the spot where her former tow partner, the MYRON, (see pp. 427-434) went down 18 months earlier. At the time of loss, the MIZTEC was towed by the steamer, ZILLAH, which also ended up sinking in this area a few years later. The MIZTEC, built at Marine City, MI, in 1890, is located in 45'-50' of water, four miles WNW of Whitefish Point. LORAN: 31156.9 / 47561.2, LAT/LON: 46.48.073 / 85.04.500

MYRON --- See *The 100 Best Great Lakes Shipwrecks, Volume II*, pp. 427-434.

NESHOTO --- This 284' wooden steamer, built at Cleveland, OH, in 1889, stranded on September 27, 1908, about 2.5 miles NE of Crisp Point because of forest fire smoke blinding the crew, all of whom were saved. This wreck is in 15'. LORAN: 31181.2 / 47527.4

NIAGARA --- All nine lives aboard this 205' schooner-barge were lost when the ship capsized in heavy seas on September 7, 1887, about 2.5 miles off Vermilion Point. The wreck, built in 1873 at Barcelona, NY, lies in 94'-105' of water. LORAN: 31168.3 / 47543.9, LAT/LON: 46.49.173 / 85.07.488

NIMICK, ALEX --- Six lives were lost when this 298' wooden steamer, stranded in a gale about 1.5 miles west of Vermilion Point on September 20, 1907. The wreck, launched at West Bay City, MI, in 1890, lies broken in 15'-22' of water. LORAN: 31203.3 / 47555.2

OSBORN, JOHN M. --- See *The 100 Best Great Lakes Shipwrecks, Vol. I*, Appendix C: 100 Deep Great Lakes Shipwrecks, pp. 258-259.

PANTHER --- See *The 100 Best Great Lakes Shipwrecks, Volume II*, pp. 435-437.

SAGAMORE --- See *The 100 Best Great Lakes Shipwrecks, Volume II*, pp. 443-446.

SUPERIOR CITY --- See *The 100 Best Great Lakes Shipwrecks, Vol. I*, Appendix C: 100 Deep Great Lakes Shipwrecks, p. 259.

THOMPSON, SADIE --- This large workbarge, built in the 1890's, was used in the construction of the Whitefish Point Harbor of refuge in the 1950's when a storm took it out of the harbor and sank it. This wreck, located in 1993 by Tom Farnquist and Dave Trotter, rests almost upside-down in 85'-116' of water about six miles south of Whitefish Point. LORAN: 31150.1 / 47619.8, LAT/LON: 46.42.537 / 84.59.878

VIENNA --- See *The 100 Best Great Lakes Shipwrecks, Volume II*, pp. 457-462.

ZILLAH --- See *The 100 Best Great Lakes Shipwrecks, Vol. I*, Appendix C: 100 Deep Great Lakes Shipwrecks, p. 259.

APPENDIX F

100 More Great Lakes Shipwrecks

Alphabetically arranged according to each of the Great Lakes, these 100 or so shipwrecks are not among the "100 best," nor are they deeper than 130', the recommended sport diving limit, nor are they within the boundaries of any underwater park or preserve. However, each Great Lakes state and province has laws against the removal of anything from any shipwreck, whether that shipwreck is in a park or a preserve, or not. Our historic Great Lakes shipwrecks are not renewable. Please leave them exactly as you find them.

Lake Ontario Shipwrecks

ALOHA/EFFIE MAE --- The 173' schooner-barge, ALOHA, built at Mt. Clemens, Michigan, in 1888, foundered in 55' of water off Nine Mile Point, Simcoe Island, near Kingston, Ontario, with the loss of her captain on October 29, 1917. The 1980's scuba charter boat, EFFIE MAE, 40' in length, was scuttled next to the ALOHA on October 17, 1993. LORAN: 15715.2 / 60034.3

ATLASCO --- This 218' wooden steamer, launched at Buffalo, NY, in 1881 as the RUSSELL SAGE, sank in a violent storm on August 7, 1921, in 43' of water off Ostrander Pt, Ontario, with no lives lost. LORAN: 15968.0 / 59996.9, LAT/LON: 43.52.76 / 76.58.90 (See underwater photo next page.)

CORNWALL --- Scuttled 7 miles west of Kingston, Ontario, in 1930, this 176' iron-hulled paddlewheeler, built at Montreal in 1855, lies in 73' of water. LORAN: 15742.2 / 60028.5, LAT/LON: 44.08.02 / 76.37.08

FABIOLA --- Off the SE corner of False Duck Island, Ontario, the wreck of this 95', 1852, two-masted schooner which sank with a coal cargo but no lives lost on October 23, 1900, lies in 55' of water. LAT/LON: 56.52 / 76.47.38

FLORENCE --- Lying in 50' of water about 300' off Timber Island near Point Traverse, Ontario, this 91' wooden tug, built in Quebec in 1885, foundered on November 14, 1933, with no lives lost. LAT/LON: 43.57.49 / 76.49.00

JAMIESON, WILLIAM --- This 100' schooner, built at Deseronto, ON, in 1878, foundered with a coal cargo in 80' off the north shore of Amherst Island, ON, with no lives lost during a storm on May 15, 1923. LORAN: 15781.55 / 59986.62

JUNO --- This 139'7" oak-hulled steamer lies in 12' of water just west of Bowmanville, Ontario, where she was used as a dock and abandoned in about 1920. LAT/LON: 43.53.01 / 78.80.02

Diver Doug Pettingill, the first person to explore the wreck of the steamer, ATLASCO, *after commercial fisherman Doug Harrison told him about this net obstruction in 1990, peers out between the spokes of the ship's wheel.*   PHOTO BY CRIS KOHL.

MACDONALD, JOHN A. --- Broken and scattered in 8' of water at the mouth of Presqu'ile Bay, ON, this old (1841), two-masted, 112' schooner stranded and broke up with no lives lost on November 17, 1872. LAT/LON: 44.08.34 / 76.35.15

MARY KAY --- This 1957, 55' tug foundered on September 21, 1988, just west of Oswego, New York, harbor in 42' of water. The two men on board were rescued. LORAN: 16094.77 / 28669.81, LAT/LON: 43.27.705 / 76.33.198

MERRILL, JULIA B. --- Burned as a public spectacle in Toronto, Ontario, in July, 1931, this 125', three-masted schooner, built in 1872, lies in 60' of water near the mouth of the Humber River. LAT/LON: 43.37.05 / 79.26.80

MILLS, DAVID W. --- This 202' 1874 wooden steamer stranded on Ford Shoals near Oswego, NY, on August 11, 1919, because of the smoke from forest fires in Canada. The remains lie in 25' of water. LAT/LON: 43.26.630 / 76.35.089.

RAE, R.H. --- This 137', three-masted bark, built at St. Catharines, Ontario, in 1857, capsized and sank during a white squall on August 3, 1858, south of Point

Traverse, Ontario. The wreck lies in 105' of water. LORAN: 15932.2 / 60032.8, LAT/LON: 43.53.136 / 76.50.340

The carved bow of the bark, R.H. RAE, *is examined by diver Marcy McElmon. This wreck is also infamous for the fact that the Jacques Cousteau expedition of 1980, on their only visit to the Great Lakes ever, lost a diver here.*   PHOTO BY CRIS KOHL.

SLIGO --- Built in 1860 at St. Catharines, ON, this 138' schooner-barge sank in 68' of water in a fierce gale on Sept. 5, 1918. LAT/LON: 43.36.640/79.27.275

WALKER, IDA --- The twin-masted schooner, IDA WALKER, attempted to enter the mouth of Weller's Bay, near Presqu'ile Point, Ontario, during a storm on November 19, 1886, but stranded and broke up on a shoal. No lives were lost. The depth is 10' - 12'. LAT/LON: 44.00.57 / 77.36.22 (old system)

Lake Erie Shipwrecks

ADVENTURE --- This 108' steamer burned on October 7, 1903, and sits in 25' of water 100' from shore in North Bay of Kelley's Island, OH, No lives were lost. LORAN: 43688.15 / 57000.89, LAT/LON: 41.38.828 / 82.41.733

ALGERIA--- This 288' schooner-barge, built at West Bay City, MI, in 1896, foundered on May 9, 1906, with 1 life lost, 1 mile north of Cleveland Harbor in 40' of water. LORAN: 43783.62 / 57482.18, LAT/LON: 41.31.222 / 81.42.940

ALVA B. --- This 73' 6" tug stranded in a storm on Thursday, November 1, 1917, 1 mile west of Avon Point, OH, approx. 100 yards off shore in 12' of water. LORAN: 43733.13 / 57314.62, LAT/LON: 41.30.771 / 82.01.891

BARR, H.A. --- Built in 1893 at West Bay City, MI, this 217' schooner-barge foundered in a storm off Rondeau, ON, on August 24, 1902, in 84' of water. LORAN: 44118.3 / 57803.2, LAT/LON: 42.09.112 / 81.23.412

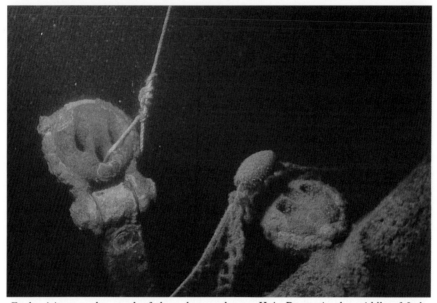

Early visitors to the wreck of the schooner-barge, H.A. BARR, *in the middle of Lake Erie, unwisely tied off a float/mooring line to a deadeye along the port rail, a use which could have damaged the piece of hardwood history. Since this photo was taken in the mid-1980's, zebra mussels have covered the deadeyes.* PHOTO BY CRIS KOHL.

BOYCE, ISABELLA J. --- Stranded and burned on Wednesday, June 6, 1917, on East Point Reef off Middle Bass Island, OH, this 138' sandsucker lies scattered in 10' to 30' of water. LAT/LON: 41.42.25 / 82.46.81

BRITON --- This 296' steel steamer, built in 1891 at Cleveland, OH, stranded and broke up off Point Abino, ON, on November 13, 1929, in 13' of water; all 27 people on board were saved. LAT/LON: 42.49.93 / 79.06.01

CASCADE --- tug, cut by ice on Sun., January 24, 1904, 200' off Lorain's west breakwall, in 30', LORAN: 43693.05 / 57221.09

CASE --- 286' steamer, stranded in a storm 600' of NW side of East Sister Island, ON, in 20', LORAN: 43742.32 / 56956.62, LAT/LON: 41.48.618 / 82.51.681

CEI BARGE --- This barge sank in the 1920's in 15'-25' about 100' north of the Avon Lake, Ohio, CEI (Cleveland Electric Illuminating Co.) wall. LORAN: 43728.14 / 57301.17

CHARGER --- 136' schooner, in Pelee Passage west of Point Pelee, sank in a collision on Thurs., July 31, 1890, now in 35', LORAN: 43812.69 / 57141.22

CLEVECO --- Lost with all hands (18) when she foundered on December 3, 1942, this 260' tanker barge was towed by the tug, ADMIRAL (see *Vol. I,* pp. 65-68) which also sank with all hands. The CLEVECO lies upside-down in 63'-77' of water. LORAN: 43926.18 / 57609.49, LAT/LON: 41.47.468 / 81.36.006

CLEVELAND, H.G. --- This 137' schooner, built in 1867 at Lorain, OH, foundered with a stone cargo after springing a leak on Aug. 14, 1899, about four miles off Lakewood, OH, in 55'. No lives were lost. LORAN: 43775.55 / 57436.12

COLGATE, JAMES B. --- With her captain alone surviving the Black Friday Storm of Oct. 20, 1916, this 308' whaleback lies upside-down in 85' 9 miles SW of Erieau, ON. LORAN: 44032.52 / 57607.72, GPS: 42.05.378 / 81.44.281

COLONIAL --- This 244' wooden steamer stranded and broke up in 14'-20' of water 7 miles west of Erieau, ON, on Nov. 13, 1914, with no lives lost. This wreck was found by Roy Pickering in May, 1991. LORAN: 44042.52 / 57472.53

CONCORD, CITY OF --- This 135' steamer, carrying coal, foundered in a storm on Saturday, September 29, 1906, and sank in 45' of water about ten miles north of Huron, OH, with the loss of two lives. LORAN: 43675.0 / 57052.7

COOK, COLONEL --- Formerly named the AUGUSTA and infamous for colliding with the sidewheel passenger steamer, LADY ELGIN, on Sept. 8, 1860 off Winnetka, IL, in which 300 lives were lost, this schooner-barge sprang a leak and sank on Sept. 23, 1894, about a quarter mile off Avon Lake, OH, and lies broken and scattered in 9'-18' of water. LORAN: 43730.48 / 57308.16

CRAFTSMAN --- This 90' barge, built at Lorain, OH in 1921, foundered on Tuesday, June 3, 1958, about one mile north of Avon Lake, OH, in 42' of water. LORAN: 43745.64 / 57332.59, LAT/LON: 41.31.938 / 82.00.370

DAVIS, CHARLES H. --- This 145' wooden steamer, foundered in a storm on June 13, 1903, about a mile north of Cleveland harbor. The wreck lies in 38'-42' of water. LORAN: 43778.57 / 57475.69, LAT/LON: 41.30.777 / 81.43.515

EXCHANGE --- This was a 138' schooner built in 1857 at Vermilion, OH, and stranded and broken up 200' south of Kelly's Island, OH, on Saturday, Nov. 28, 1874, with the remains scattered in 8'-22'. LORAN: 43672.18 / 56973.97

FINCH --- This 105' scow, usually towed by the tug, A.I. HOLLOWAY, sank on August 2, 1883, in 43'. No lives were lost. LAT/LON: 42.50.99 / 78.59.06

GRAND TRAVERSE --- Broken and scattered on a silty bottom in 40' of water 3 miles SE of Colchester, ON, this 181' wooden steamer sank in a collision with the steamer, LIVINGSTONE, on October 19, 1896. LORAN: 43795.92 / 56975.11

GRIFFIN, JOHN B. --- This 57' tug sank after burning to the waterline on Tuesday, July 12, 1892, about two miles off Lakewood, OH, and lies on a starboard angle in 46'-53' of water. No lives were lost. LORAN: 43767.15 / 57427.39

HICKORY STICK --- This 110', 1944 dredge sank during a storm in 52'-57' of water on November 29, 1958, while being towed by the tug, BLACK MARLIN, about three miles north of Sheffield Lake, OH. Both tug and tow sank after the towline parted; the tug has yet to be found. No lives were lost. The crane, boiler, and hull form the most conspicuous items at this site. LORAN: 43733.88 / 57282.82, LAT/LON: 41.32.299 / 82.06.241

IVANHOE --- This old schooner, built in 1848 and measuring 110' x 25' 9" x 9' 3", sank in 58' of water after a collision with the schooner, ARAB, on Thursday, October 4, 1855, about three miles off Avon Lake, OH. No lives were lost. LORAN: 43750.16 / 57316.92, LAT/LON: 41.33.306 / 82.02.830

JONES, FANNIE L. --- Lying scattered in 37' of water almost a mile NW of Cleveland Harbor, this 93' scow-schooner foundered in a storm on August 10, 1890. LORAN: 4377703 / 57473.11, LAT/LON: 41.30.636 / 81.43.747

LUEDTKE, DUKE --- This 68' tug, built at Cleveland in 1917 and used in the attempted salvage of the PRINS WILLEM V in Lake Michigan in the mid-1960's, sprang a leak and sank 13 miles north of Avon Point, OH, on Sept. 21, 1993, with 1 life lost. The wreck sits in mud on a port list, the stern buried, in 65'-71'. LORAN: 43825.54 / 57396.29, LAT/LON: 41.41.628 / 81.57.651.

LYCOMING --- This 251' wooden steamer, built at West Bay City, MI, in 1880, burned and sank 4 miles east of Erieau, Ontario, harbor entrance, on October 21, 1910, with no loss of life. The wreck sits in 28' of water. LORAN: 44073.02 / 57566.43, LAT/LON: 42.15.075 / 81.53.385

LYON, JOHN B. --- In 50' 5 miles north of Conneaut, OH, this 256' wooden steamer lies on its side. The LYON foundered in a severe gale on Sept. 12, 1900, with the loss of 10 of the 16 people on board. LORAN: 44222.35 / 58211.96

MECOSTA --- This 282' wooden steamer, built at West Bay City, MI, in 1888, was scuttled in 1922 3 miles north of Bay Village, OH, in 50' of water. LORAN: 43763.32 / 57397.34, LAT/LON: 41.31.854 / 81.52.997

MEYER, F.A. --- Cut by ice, this 256' wooden steamer sank in 80' with no lives lost on Dec. 18, 1909, in the middle of Lake Erie between Erieau, ON, and Avon Point, OH. LORAN: 43912.03 / 57406.42, GPS: 41.55.441 / 82.02.952

NEW BRUNSWICK --- In 48'-54' of water 4 miles south of Port Alma, ON, this 129' bark foundered in a gale on August 26, 1858, with a cargo of oak and black walnut, and 5 of 9 lives lost. LORAN: 43950.93 / 57321.19

NORTH CAROLINA --- This 75' tug sprang a leak and sank on December 9, 1968, in about 40' of water almost a mile off Mentor-on-the-Lake, OH. No lives were lost. LORAN: 43934.27 / 57709.27, LAT/LON: 41.43.801 / 81.22.888

OSBORNE --- This bark, built in 1867, stranded off Point Abino, ON, on Nov. 3, 1874 and was abandoned. She lies in 10'-13'. LAT/LON: 42.51.93 / 79.56.45

PRIDGEON, JOHN, JR. --- Lying on its port side in 55'-62' 5 miles NE of Avon Point, OH, this 221' wooden steamer sprang a leak and foundered on Sept. 18, 1909. LORAN: 43775.71 / 57362.29, LAT/LON: 41,35.316 / 81.58.597

RALEIGH --- This 227' wooden steamer foundered off Point Abino, ON, on November 30, 1911, in 30' with no loss of lives. LAT/LON: 42.34.892 / 79.56.455

REED, JAMES H. --- This 455' steel steamer, built in 1903, sank in a collision with the steamer, ASHCROFT, on the foggy night of April 27, 1944, off Port Stanley, ON. Twelve lives were lost. This huge wreck lies dynamited in 70' of water. LORAN: 44278.03 / 58139.55

ROBERT --- This 45' fish tug sank in 50' of water after a collision with another fish tug on Sept. 26, 1982, 5 miles south of Erieau, ON., with no lives lost. LORAN: 44044.15 / 57510.47, LAT/LON: 42.13.090 / 82.58.940

SAND MERCHANT --- This 252' steel sandsucker sank in 65' 4 miles NE of Avon Point, OH, on Oct. 17, 1936, with 19 lives lost. The wreck lies upside-down. LORAN: 43771.77 / 57368.32, LAT/LON: 41.34.431 / 82.57.520

STEEL PRODUCTS ---Launched in 1901 at Lorain, OH, as the VENUS, this 350' vessel ran aground in 1960 near Point Abino, ON, with some of the wreck above water. A four-bladed propeller remains. LAT/LON: 42.51.74 / 79.08.39

VALENTINE --- This 128' schooner, built at Conneaut, OH, in 1867, foundered in 80' of water in mid-lake off Erieau, ON, on October 10, 1877, with no lives lost. LORAN: 43931.37 / 57476.32, GPS: 41.55.122 / 81.54.786

VIGOR, FRANK E. --- Upside-down in 92' and pointing north, this 418' steel steamer sank in a collision with the steamer, PHILIP MINCH, on April 27, 1944, with no lives lost. LORAN: 43942.03 / 57464.44, GPS: 41.57.549 / 81.57.238

WILMA --- This fishing tug sank 9 miles off Port Dover, ON, towards Long Point, when ice cut through the wooden hull in the spring of 1936. The wreck sits upright and intact in 75' of water. LORAN: 44607.4 / 58620.1

WILSON, ANNABELLE ---This 174' schooner-barge foundered in 60' of water on July 12, 1913, off Dunkirk, NY, with 2 lives lost. LAT/LON: 42.29.911 / 79.21.117

WILSON, MABEL --- This 242' schooner foundered in 38' of water on May 28, 1906; 1 life lost. LORAN: 43774.24 / 57470.48, LAT/LON: 41.30.333 / 81.43.913

Lake Huron Shipwrecks

AZTEC/PROVINCE --- The remains of these two ships lay rotting in Sarnia harbor until the 1936 clean-up, when the dynamited AZTEC was placed aboard the refloated hull of the PROVINCE and both were scuttled in lower Lake Huron. The 189' wooden steamer, AZTEC, was destroyed by fire on November 9, 1923, at Marine City, MI, before being towed to Sarnia. The 166' barge, PROVINCE capsized in the St. Clair River on Sept. 28, 1923, with 3 lives lost. She was raised, towed to Sarnia, and abandoned. The shipwrecks, now in 68', were found and identified by Jim Stayer and Cris Kohl in 1993. LORAN: 30770.5 / 49618.3, LAT/LON: 43.09.83 / 82.18.49

BURLINGTON --- This 137' wooden steamer burned at Mississagi Straits Lighthouse, western Manitoulin Island, on August 24, 1895, with no lives lost. The remains lie in 23', accessible from shore. LAT/LON: 45.53.53 / 83.13.34

CANISTEO --- Located and identified in 1997 by Jim and Pat Stayer, Tim Juhl, David Fritz, and Cris Kohl, this 182' wooden steamer was scuttled in 98' north of Port Huron, MI, on October 25, 1920. LAT/LON: 43.14.142 / 82.18.292

CAROLINE ROSE --- Marked with a buoy each spring, this 132' Nova Scotia schooner, scuttled in Driftwood Cove in 58' of water 300' off shore just outside Fathom Five National Marine Park boundaries on August 27, 1990, was the second commercial ship scuttled in the Great Lakes as a new scuba dive site.

The East Coast schooner, CAROLINE ROSE, *was purposely scuttled in 1990 to create a new scuba dive site near Tobermory, ON. Here, diver Joan Forsberg explores the wreckage, including some ornamental wood trim from the bow.* PHOTO BY CRIS KOHL.

CRANAGE, THOMAS ---In 25' off "The Watchers" Islands in S Georgian Bay, this 305' wooden steamer stranded here with no lives lost on Sept. 25, 1911. LORAN: 29593.6 / 48906.0, LAT/LON: 44.56.39 / 80.05.27 (old system)

GOUDREAU --- This 300' steel steamer, stranded on a reef south of Lyal Island near Stokes Bay, ON, on November 23, 1917, broke up in place with no lives lost. Much of this steel was salvaged for the war effort in 1942, but much remains in place in 18'-28' of water. LAT/LON: 46.03.45 / 82.12.55

MICHIGAN --- Built at West Bay City, MI, in 1890, this 296' steel barge stranded off the NW side of Hope Island in lower Georgian Bay on Nov. 24, 1943, and broke up with no lives lost. The wreck lies scattered in 10'-15'. LORAN: 29637.73 / 48912.73, LAT/LON: 44.54.58 / 80.12.15 (old system)

A winch with braided steel cable offers one of many photographic opportunities at the shallow GOUDREAU *wreck site south of Lyal Island, Ontario.* PHOTO BY CRIS KOHL.

The broken remains of the wooden steamer, SEATTLE, *lie in shallow water a fair distance from the nearest town of Parry Sound, ON. This site provides a clear opportunity to see nautical items such as a steering quadrant.* PHOTO BY CRIS KOHL.

MIDLAND --- This 62' wooden tug, built in 1896 in Midland, ON, foundered in 1923 in 50' of water west of Parry Sound, ON. LORAN: 29708.44 / 48718.55

SACHEM --- Built in 1889, this 187' wooden steamer burned in the St. Clair River on October 8, 1928, and was scuttled in 68' of water in lower Lake Huron six weeks later. LORAN: 30769.2 / 49617.6, LAT/LON: 43.09.91 / 82.18.31

SAN JACINTO --- This 265-ton schooner, launched in 1856 at Buffalo, NY, foundered off Yeo Island north of Tobermory, ON, on June 20, 1881, with no lives lost. Found by Paul LaPointe in 1990, this wreck sits broken in 80' of water. LORAN: 30242.7 / 48619.1, LAT/LON: 45.24.27 / 81.47.72

SEATTLE --- Lying in 15'-25' of water just west of Green Island, in the Mink Islands, Georgian Bay, west of Parry Sound, ON, this 160' wooden steamer, built in 1892 at Oscoda, MI, stranded here in heavy seas on November 11, 1903, and broke up in place, with no lives lost. LORAN: 29735.66 / 48706.82

Diver Jim Stayer, part of the team which first located and identified the historic steamer, YAKIMA, *videotapes the immense wooden hull.* PHOTO BY CRIS KOHL.

SWEETHEART --- These shipwreck remains, lying in 30' of water 3 miles north of Sarnia, ON, are considered to be those of this 176' schooner. LORAN: 30834.1 / 49671.8, LAT/LON: 43.02.45 / 82.23.15

WAUBUNO --- In 10'-20' of water just off S Bradden Island, SSW of Parry Sound, ON, this wooden paddlewheeler foundered with all hands (30) on Nov. 22, 1879, and drifted to this cove. LAT/LON: 45.07.15 / 80.09.58 (old system)

WAWINET --- This 87' private yacht foundered on Sept. 21, 1942; 25 of 42 on board died. The wreck sits upright in 25' of water N of Penetanguishene, ON. LORAN: 29501.9 / 48970.7, LAT/LON: 44.49.30 / 79.05.54 (old system)

WOLFE, LOTTIE --- This three-masted, 126' schooner stranded off the NE corner of Hope Island in lower Georgian Bay with a corn cargo on Oct. 16, 1891, with no lives lost. The remains lie broken in 18'. LORAN: 29501.92 / 48914.33

YAKIMA --- This 279' wooden steamer, the first commercial ship on the Great Lakes to be equipped with electric lights, stranded and burned in the St. Clair River on June 10, 1905, and towed to Sarnia Bay, abandoned, and scuttled in Lake Huron in 1928. Located and identified in 1993 by Jim and Pat Stayer, Tim Juhl, David Fritz, and Cris Kohl, this wreck sits in 78' 11 miles N of Port Huron, MI. LORAN: 30775.1 / 49612.6, LAT/LON: 43.10.56 / 82.19.38

Lake Michigan Shipwrecks

ADVANCE --- This twin-masted, 117' schooner foundered 9 miles south of Sheboygan, WI, on September 8, 1885, with all hands (6). It sits in 83' of water. LORAN: 32741.2 / 48919.3, LAT/LON: 43.36.71 / 87.49.91

AMERICA --- This three-masted, 137' schooner sank in a collision with two stone scows towed by the tugs *Gagnon* and *A.W. Lawrence* on September 29, 1880. The wreck lies in 125' of water off the Kewaunee, WI, Nuclear Power Plant. LORAN: 32423.2 / 48498.7, LAT/LON: 44.21.02 / 87.26.82

APPOMATOX --- This 319' wooden steamer stranded on November 2, 1905, 400' south of the first north pier, Atwater Beach, Whitefish Bay, WI, N of Milwaukee, in 20'. LORAN: 32969.3 / 49231.1, LAT/LON: 43.95.53 / 76.52.11

ATLANTA --- Lying bow north 500' off shore in 14'-20' of water, this wooden, 200' steamer burned and beached on March 16, 1906, 14 miles S of Sheboygan, WI. LORAN: 32772.6 / 48933.5, LAT/LON: 43.34.23 / 76.46.89

BALDWIN, S.C. --- This 160' wooden towbarge foundered on September 3, 1908 with 1 life lost, in 80' of water 2 miles SE of Rawley Pt., just north of Two Rivers, WI. LORAN: 32487.7 / 48597.8, LAT/LON: 44.10.90 / 87.29.09

BOAZ --- This 114', three-masted schooner, built in 1869, sank in 15' of water in North Bay, near Bailey's Harbor, WI, after waiting out a storm on November 10, 1900. LORAN: 32082.42 / 48093.79, LAT/LON: 45.08.31 / 87.03.08

BROWN, W.L. --- This 140' wooden steamer foundered in a gale off Peshtigo, WI, on October 21, 1886. The wreck sits upright and intact in 80', often with poor visibility. LORAN: 32261.6 / 48096.8, LAT/LON: 44.57.96 / 87.33.05

CAR FERRY BARGE #2 --- This 310' railroad car ferry was scuttled in 1907 and dynamited. Today, she lies scattered in 42' about 3 miles off the Calumet breakwall. LORAN: 33407.62 / 50205.74, LAT/LON: 41.44.82 / 87.26.98

CARRINGTON --- This 215' schooner stranded and broke up on Hat Island Reef off Egg Harbor, WI, on October 30, 1870, with a load of pig iron and shingles. The wreck lies broken in 35' to 55'. Beware of the boulder that is awash next to the wreck. LORAN: 32167.42 / 48067.39, LAT/LON: 45.05.58 / 87.19.33

CHERUBUSCO --- This 144' bark, built in 1848 in Milwaukee and stranded in North Bay, WI, in November, 1872, with no lives lost, lies in 10' of water. LORAN: 32084.5 / 48090.2, LAT/LON: 45.08.46 / 87.03.71

CIRCASSIAN --- This 135' schooner, stranded with grain on Nov. 22, 1860, on White Shoals, near Mackinac, with no lives lost. The broken remains lie in 12'. LORAN: 31356.6 / 48033.7, LAT/LON: 45.50.09 / 85.09.22

CORT, HENRY --- Lying broken, scattered, and often buoyed near the north Muskegon, MI, breakwall in 48'-55' of water, this 320' 1892 steel whaleback crashed into it on November 30, 1934. One Coast Guard rescuer lost his life.

DOWS, DAVID --- This famous, 265' schooner, the only five-masted ship on the Great Lakes, built at Toledo, OH, in 1881, foundered in 45' of water off South Chicago, IL, on Nov. 29, 1889, with no lives lost. LORAN: 33383.6 / 50201.7, LAT/LON: 41.45.95 / 87.23.58

ELGIN, LADY --- This 252' sidewheel steamer sank in a collision off Winnetka, IL, on Sept. 8, 1869; 300 people died. This wreck is reportedly off-limits while the salvage case is still in litigation. Co-ordinates are on the Internet.

EUREKA --- This 240' sidewheel steamer stranded Oct. 12, 1873, in 50' off Michigan City, IN. LORAN: 33237.42 / 50281.19, LAT/LON: 41.44.27 / 86.53.06

FLEETWING --- This 136' schooner, built in 1867 at Manitowoc, WI, stranded at the tip of the Door Peninsula on Sept. 26, 1888, with no lives lost. She lies in 25' of water. LORAN: 32041.11 / 48006.22, LAT/LON: 45.17.25 / 87.02.99

GILMORE, J.E./A.P. NICHOLS/FOREST --- The 138' schooner, J.C. GILMORE, stranded at Pilot Island, WI, on Oct. 19, 1892, and the 147' schooner, A.P. NICHOLS, joined her on Oct. 28, 1892. They were both exactly where the 88' scow-schooner, FOREST, had stranded on Oct. 28, 1891. No lives were lost. The remains of these 3 ships lie in 20'-50' of water. LORAN: 32006.5 / 48032.3, LAT/LON: 45.17.16 / 86.55.23

GUST, HENRY --- This 72' wooden tug, built in Milwaukee in 1893, was shortened by 10' in 1929 and scuttled in 1935. She lies in 80' with boiler and prop highlights, off Two Rivers, WI. LORAN: 32501.1 / 48619.9

HACKETT, R.J. --- This 208' steamer burned and stranded on Whaleback Shoal in Green Bay, WI, on Nov. 12, 1905, with a coal cargo. No lives were lost. She lies in 10'-30'. LORAN: 32057.7 / 47938.8, LAT/LON: 45.21.42 / 87.11.00

HILL, FLORA M. --- This 130' wooden steamer, built in 1874 at Philadelphia, PA, was sunk by ice in 37' of water off Chicago on March 11, 1912. No lives were lost LORAN: 33375.4 / 50077.0, LAT/LON: 41.54.34 / 87.35.08

HINTON, FRANCIS --- This 152' wooden steamer, built at Manitowoc, WI, in 1889, stranded and broke up off Two Rivers, WI, on Nov. 16, 1909, with no lives lost. She lies in 20' with boiler, prop, etc. LORAN: 32548.92 / 48614.32

ILLINOIS --- This hydraulic dredge, reputedly the largest on the Great Lakes at the time, sank on December 9, 1907, in 34' of water south of Chicago. LORAN: 33403.1 / 50128.4, LAT/LON: 41.49.99 / 87.34.26

IOWA --- Ice broke in the wooden hull of this 202' steamer on Feb. 4, 1915, 2 miles off Chicago Light. The ship sank in 35', but no lives were lost. LORAN: 33373.7 / 50087.1, LAT/LON: 41.53.76 / 87.33.76

KELLY, KATE --- This 126' schooner foundered off Racine, WI, in 54' of water, on May 14, 1895, with all hands (7) and a cargo of railroad ties. LORAN: 33053.5 / 49467.3, LAT/LON: 42.46.56 / 87.45.45

KEUKA --- This 172' schooner-barge sits in 50' of water at Charlevoix, MI, where it was scuttled in the 1930's. LORAN: 31495.6 / 48304.4, LAT/LON: 45.18.34 / 84.59.99

LOUISIANA --- No lives were lost, but this 267' steamer burned to a total loss while at anchor during the Great Storm of November 9, 1913, at Washington Island, WI. The wreck lies in 2'-20' of water. LORAN: 31975.7 / 47964.9, LAT/LON: 45.24.10 / 86.55.24

LOUISVILLE --- This 140' wooden steamer burned and sank on September 29, 1857, in 60' of water 7 miles off Calumet, IL. LORAN: 33365.9 / 50205.5, LAT/LON: 41.46.28 / 87.20.34

LYONS, DANIEL --- This 137', three-masted schooner collided with the schooner, KATE GILLETT, in October, 1878, and sank in 95' 5 miles off Wolf River, WI, with no lives lost. LORAN: 32283.5 / 48329.1, LAT/LON: 44.40.23 / 87.17.70

MARSHALL, J.D. --- This 154' wooden steamer capsized on June 10, 1911, and sank in 32' off Michigan City, IN, with the loss of 4 lives. LORAN: 33329.4 / 50309.2, LAT/LON: 41.40.04 / 87.04.21

MCMULLEN AND PITZ DREDGE --- Located by Steve Radovan in 1984, this dredge sank in a storm off Cleveland, WI, on Nov. 18, 1919, in 85' of water. LORAN: 32632.7 / 48746.5, LAT/LON: 43.53.52 / 87.40.31

MERIDIEN --- This two-masted schooner stranded off the south end of Little Sister Island in Green Bay, WI, in October, 1873. She lies in 35'-45' of water. LORAN : 32084.1 / 48030.2, LAT/LON: 45.12.81 / 87.08.57

MICHIGAN, STATE OF --- This 165' wooden steamer foundered in 77' of water about 2 miles NW of Whitehall, MI, on Oct. 18, 1901, with no lives lost. LORAN: 32453.9 / 49263.4, LAT/LON: 43.23.20 / 86.27.91

MILWAUKEE --- This 185' steamer sank with no lives lost in a collision with the schooner, J.H. TIFFANY, which also sank, on November 29, 1859, 5 miles SW of Grays Reef Light, MI. This wreck sits in 96' of water. LORAN: 31407.2 / 48077.8, LAT/LON: 45.43.50 / 85.14.85

MINCH, ANNA C. --- This 380' steel steamer foundered with all hands (24) and a coal cargo 1.5 miles south of Pentwater, MI, during the severe Armistice Day Storm of November 11, 1940. This enormous wreck lies in 45' of water. Bow: LORAN: 32326.3 / 49029.9 LAT/LON: 43.45.68 / 86.27.79. Stern: LORAN: 32327.1 / 49030.7, LAT/LON: 43.45.60 / 86.27.87

MUSKEGON --- This old, 211' wooden steamer burned at her dock at Michigan City, IN, on Oct. 16, 1910, and was scuttled off shore 8 months later. She lies in 25' of water. LORAN: 33266.0 / 50293.5, LAT/LON: 41.42.71 / 86.56.15

NEFF, SIDNEY O. --- This 160' wooden steamer was scuttled in June, 1940, in 15' of water a quarter of a mile south of the Marinette, WI, lighthouse. LORAN: 32233.22 / 48015.22, LAT/LON: 45.05.52 / 87.34.62

NOVADOC --- Stranded and broken up off Pentwater, MI, during the Armistice Day Storm of Nov. 11, 1940, with 2 lives lost, this 235' steel steamer lies in 12'-15'. LORAN: 32366.2 / 49064.4, LAT/LON: 43.41.61 / 86.31.08

PATHFINDER --- This 188', three-masted schooner stranded N of Two Rivers, WI, on Nov. 19, 1886, with iron ore and no lives lost. She lies broken in 10' of water. LORAN: 32473.56 / 48552.36, LAT/LON: 44.14.69 / 87.30.69

PRIDE --- This 87' schooner lies broken and scattered in 40' of water at the N end of Washington Island. She stranded there on Nov. 29, 1901, with no lives lost. LORAN: 31975.12 / 47963.45, LAT/LON: 45.29.82 / 86.38.82

RAINBOW --- This 125' schooner, built at Buffalo, NY, in 1855, foundered off Chicago on May 18, 1894, and lies broken up in 20'. LORAN: 33397.5 / 50098.5, LAT/LON: 41.52.10 / 87.36.46

RIVERSIDE --- This 133' schooner, built at Oswego, NY, in 1870, capsized in a storm and sank in 1887 300' south of Pilot Island, WI, resting upside-down in 45' (stern) to 60' (bow), with wreckage spilled to 100'. LORAN: 32009.7 / 48034.4, LAT/LON: 45.16.70 / 86.55.72

ROEN --- This steam barge, owned by salvager John Roen, sank in heavy seas 3 miles south of Poverty Island in 1956 in 110' of water. The wreck is upside-down supported by the crane. The tug towing this barge also sank and lies nearby. LORAN: 31885.02 / 47967.79, LAT/LON: 45.28.74 / 86.40.22 and also LORAN: 31889.7 / 47964.4, LAT/LON: 45.28.82 / 86.41.09

SALVOR --- This 253' barge foundered on Sept. 16, 1930, with all hands (5) and a stone cargo. The remains lie in 28' of water 3 miles N of the Muskegon, MI, lighthouse. LORAN: 32467.1 / 49356.0, LAT/LON: 43.15.49 / 86.22.19

SCOTT, WINFIELD --- Capsized off Hog Island, WI, in a gale on Aug. 30, 1871, this two-masted schooner stranded there and broke up in 7'-10' with no lives lost. LORAN: 31968.53 / 48000.22, LAT/LON: 45.21.74 / 86.51.38

SEBASTOPOL --- This new, 245' sidewheel steamer stranded at S. Milwaukee pier on Sept. 18, 1855, with the loss of 4 lives. The wreck lies in 10'-15' inside the breakwater. LORAN: 33008.7 / 49304.3, LAT/LON: 42.58.93 / 87.51.75

STONE, WILLIAM --- This 108' schooner stranded with a lumber cargo in Cecil Bay at the Straits of Mackinac on Oct. 13, 1901. The broken remains lie scattered in 10'. LORAN: 31270.7 / 48128.2, LAT/LON: 45.44.90 / 84.30.05

TIFFANY, J.H. --- This 137' schooner sank with 5 lives and a cargo of rail iron 5 miles SW of Grays Reef Light, MI, after a collision with the steamer, MILWAUKEE, which also sank, on November 29, 1859. The wreck sits in 103' of water. LORAN: 31402.0 / 48081.7, LAT/LON: 45.43.37 / 85.13.76

VOLUNTEER --- This 271' wooden steamer was dismantled and burned in 1914 at South Point, Milwaukee, WI. The wreck lies in 13'-15' on both sides of the breakwall. LORAN: 33008.7 / 49304.3, LAT/LON: 42.59.19 / 87.51.51

WHEELER, FRANK W. --- This 256' wooden steamer stranded in a snowstorm on Dec. 3, 1893, E of Michigan City, IN. The remains lie 1200' off shore in 30'-40' of water. LORAN: 33228.7 / 50278.9, LAT/LON: 41.44.64 / 86.51.98

WILLIAMS, GEORGE F. --- Abandoned off Chicago in 1913, this 294' wooden steamer, built at West Bay City, MI, in 1889, lies in 20' with the engine, boiler and prop in place. LORAN: 33338.8 / 49970.2, LAT/LON: 42.02.67 / 87.40.14

WINGS OF THE WIND --- This 130' schooner sank with a cargo of coal in a collision with the schr., H.P. BALDWIN, in 40' N of Chicago on May 12, 1866, with no lives lost. LORAN: 33357.5 / 50064.1, LAT/LON: 41.55.86 / 87.33.50

WINSLOW, KATE --- This 202' schooner, launched in 1872 at West Bay City, MI, stranded on October 14, 1897, off Point Seul Choix, MI, and eventually sank in 85' of water. LORAN: 31356.42 / 48026.44

WINSLOW, RICHARD --- This huge, 216' schooner foundered in 32' of water with iron ore and no lives lost on Sept. 5, 1898, 1.5 miles W of White Shoals Lt. near Mackinac. LORAN: 31356.5 / 48026.4, LAT/LON: 45.50.50 / 85.09.58

WISCONSIN --- This 181' wooden steamer, built in Detroit in 1882, was burned and scuttled in 1935 in 85' just N of Green Island in Green Bay, WI. LORAN: 32213.42 / 48040.19, LAT/LON: 45.04.99 / 87.29.29

Lake Superior Shipwrecks

FRYER, ROBERT L. --- This ship was burned as a public spectacle on July 29, 1930, at "B" Island in the Welcome Islands, near Thunder Bay, ON. The remains are in water up to 35' deep, with part above water. LORAN: 31801.7 / 45902.4

GRAY OAK --- This scow-schooner was scuttled in 1911 in 108' of water about 2 miles beyond the Welcome Islands near Thunder Bay, ON. The site is sometimes marked with a jug. LORAN: 31800.7 / 45915.7

MCLACHLAN, MARY E. --- This four-masted, 251' schooner, built in 1893, foundered a mile offshore, 35 miles west of Schreiber, ON, on Nov. 7, 1921, with no loss of life. LORAN: 31454.5 / 46053.0, LAT/LON: 48.54.66 / 87.48.06

NEEBING --- Five lives were lost when this 193' gravel carrier foundered off the north tip of Moss Island in the Nipigon Straits, ON, on September 24, 1937. The wreck lies in 100' of water. LAT/LON: 48.39.80 / 88.07.80

ONTARIO --- This 181' wooden steamer stranded at the E end of Battle Island on Aug. 10, 1899, with no lives lost. The wreck lies scattered off the boiler on land. LORAN: 31426.7 / 46178.0, LAT/LON: 48.45.20 / 87.31.99

PUCKASAW --- This 1889 96' steam tug was scuttled in 1911 off "B" Island in the Welcome Islands near Thunder Bay, ON. The deck sits at 55', with more wreckage to 80' of water. LORAN: 31801.4 / 45901.3

STRATHMORE --- In Shaffer Bay, at the W end of Michipicoten Island, ON, this 207' wooden steamer lies in 5'-35' of water. The ship stranded on November 14, 1906 with a grain cargo and no lives lost. LAT/LON: 47.44.64 / 85.57.36

Our human trespass must leave no marks. PHOTO BY CRIS KOHL.

BIBLIOGRAPHY

Some vain writers of history give the impression that they author their books without any research whatsoever, or they suggest that their writings, having no derivations, are completely original. Readers know that this is bunk. I do much primary material research, but my appetite for what others have written is equally voracious. I wish to share with you the food which helped nourish this book:

BOOKS

Amos, Art, and Patrick Folkes. *A Diver's Guide to Georgian Bay*. Toronto, Ontario: Ontario Underwater Council, 1979.

Arlov, Gary. *Divers Guide to the Shipwrecks of Lake Michigan*. Milwaukee, Wisconsin: The Arlov Company, 1987.

Ayare, John C., and Ward Pautler. *Shipwrecks*. Buffalo, New York: Niagara Frontier Underwater Society, Inc., 1979.

Barcus, Frank. *Freshwater Fury*. Detroit: Wayne State University Press, 1960.

Barry, James P. *Ships of the Great Lakes, 300 Years of Navigation*. Berkley, California: Howell-North Books, 1973.

_____*Wrecks and Rescues of the Great Lakes, A Photographic History*. La Jolla, California: Howell-North Books, 1981.

Berent, John. *Diving the Lake Erie Island Wrecks*. Marblehead, Ohio: John Berent, 1992.

Bors, Brian J. ed. *New York State Dive Site Directory*. Niagara Falls, New York: The New York State Divers Association, 1993 edition.

Bowen, Dana Thomas. *Lore of the Lakes*. Cleveland, Ohio: Dana Thomas Bowen, 1940.

_____*Memories of the Lakes*. Daytona Beach, Florida: Dana Thomas Bowen, 1946.

_____*Shipwrecks of the Lakes*. Cleveland, Ohio: Dana Thomas Bowen, 1952.

Boyer, Dwight. *Ghost Ships of the Great Lakes*. New York: Dodd, Mead & Co., 1968.

_____*Great Stories of the Great Lakes*. New York: Dodd, Mead & Co., 1966.

_____*Ships and Men of the Great Lakes*. New York: Dodd, Mead & Co., 1977.

_____*Strange Adventures on the Great Lakes*. New York: Dodd, Mead & Co., 1974.

_____*True Tales of the Great Lakes*. New York: Dodd, Mead & Co., 1971.

Cain, Emily. *Ghost Ships, Hamilton and Scourge: Historical Treasures from the War of 1812*. Toronto, Ontario: Musson, 1983.

Creviere, Paul J., Jr. *Wild Gales and Tattered Sails*. Paul John Creviere, Jr., 1997.

Curwood, James Oliver. *The Great Lakes: The Vessels That Plow Them, Their Owners, Their Sailors, and Their Cargoes, Together with a Brief History of Our Inland Seas*. New York: G. P. Putnam's Sons, 1909.

Feltner, Dr. Charles E. and Jeri Baron. *Shipwrecks of the Straits of Mackinac*. Dearborn, Michigan: Seajay Publications, 1991.

Frederickson, Arthur C. and Lucy F. *Pictorial History of the C. & O. Train and Auto Ferries and Pere Marquette Line Steamers*. Frankfort, Michigan: Arthur C. and Lucy F. Frederickson, 1955, rev. 1965.

_____*Ships and Shipwrecks in Door County, Wisconsin, Volume One*. Frankfort, Michigan: Arthur C. and Lucy F. Frederickson, 1961.

_____*Ships and Shipwrecks in Door County, Wisconsin, Volume Two*. Frankfort, Michigan: Arthur C. and Lucy F. Frederickson, 1963.

Frimodig, Mac. *Shipwrecks off Keweenaw*. The Fort Wilkins Natural History Association in cooperation with the Michigan Dept. of Natural Resources.

Gentile, Gary. *The Nautical Cyclopedia*. Philadelphia: Gary Gentile Productions, 1995.

Greenwood, John O. *Namesakes 1900-1909*. Cleveland, Ohio: Freshwater Press, Inc., 1987.

_____*Namesakes 1910-1919*. Cleveland, Ohio: Freshwater Press, Inc., 1986.

_____*Namesakes 1920-1929*. Cleveland, Ohio: Freshwater Press, Inc., 1984.

_____*Namesakes 1930-1955*. Cleveland, Ohio: Freshwater Press, Inc., 1978.

_____*Namesakes 1956-1980*. Cleveland, Ohio: Freshwater Press, Inc., 1981.

Halsey, John R. *Beneath the Inland Seas: Michigan's Underwater Archaeological Heritage*. Lansing: Bureau of History, Michigan Department of State, 1990.

Hammer, Patrick. *Lake Michigan Shipwrecks*. Alsip, Illinois: Scuba Emporium, 1996 (5th edition).

Harold, Steve. *Shipwrecks of the Sleeping Bear*. Traverse City, Michigan: Pioneer Study Center, 1984.

Harrington, Steve. *Divers Guide to Michigan*. Mason, Michigan: Maritime Press, 1990; revised edition, 1998.

_____with David J. Cooper. *Divers Guide to Wisconsin including Minnesota's North Shore*. Mason, Michigan: Maritime Press, 1991.

Hatcher, Harlan. *The Great Lakes*. London, New York, Toronto, Ontario: Oxford University Press, 1944.

_____*Lake Erie.* American Lakes Series. Indianapolis and New York: Bobbs-Merrill Co., 1945.

_____and Erich A. Walter. *A Pictorial History of the Great Lakes.* New York: Bonanza Books, 1963.

Heden, Karl E. *Directory of Shipwrecks of the Great Lakes.* Boston, Massachusetts: Bruce Humphries Pubs., 1966.

Hemming, Robert J. *Gales of November, The Sinking of the Edmund Fitzgerald.* Chicago: Contemporary Books, 1981.

Heyl, Eric. *Early American Steamers, Volumes I-VI.* Buffalo, New York: Eric Heyl, 1953-1969.

Hirthe, Walter M. and Mary K. *Schooner Days in Door County.* Minneapolis: Voyageur Press, Inc., 1986.

Holden, Thom. *Above and Below, A History of Lighthouses and Shipwrecks of Isle Royale.* Houghton, Michigan: Isle Royale Natural History Association, 1985.

Humphries, William. *Great Fury.* London, Ontario: William Humphries, 1975.

Johnson, Kathy, and Greg Lashbrook. *Diving and Snorkeling Guide to the Great Lakes.* Houston, Texas: Pisces Books, 1991.

Keller, James M. *The "Unholy" Apostles, Tales of Chequamegon Shipwrecks.* Bayfield, Wisconsin: Apostle Island Press, 1984.

Keefe, William F. *Voices from the Sweetwater Seas.* New Buffalo, MU: Action Research Institute, 1997.

Kemp. Peter, ed. *The Oxford Companion to Ships and the Sea.* London: Oxford University Press, 1976.

Kohl, Cris. *Dive Ontario, The Guide to Shipwrecks and Scuba.* Chatham, Ontario: Cris Kohl, 1990, revised 1995.

_____*Dive Ontario Two! More Ontario Shipwreck Stories.* Chatham, Ontario: Cris Kohl, 1994.

_____*Dive Southwestern Ontario.* Chatham, Ontario: Cris Kohl, 1985.

_____*Shipwreck Tales: The St. Clair River (to 1900).* Chatham, Ontario: Cris Kohl, 1987.

_____*Treacherous Waters: Kingston's Shipwrecks.* Chatham, Ontario: Cris Kohl, 1997.

Landon, Fred. *Lake Huron.* American Lakes Series. Indianapolis & New York: Bobbs-Merrill Company, 1944.

Lane, Kit. *Built on the Banks of the Kalamazoo.* Douglas, Michigan: Pavilion Press, 1993.

_____*Chicora, Lost on Lake Michigan.* Douglas, Michigan: Pavilion Press, 1996.

_____*"The Dustless Road to Happyland," Chicago-Saugatuck Passenger Boats, 1859-1929.* Douglas, Michigan: Pavilion Press, 1995.

_____*Shipwrecks of the Saugatuck Area.* Saugatuck, Michigan: Saugatuck Commercial Record, 1974.

Lenihan, Daniel. *Shipwrecks of Isle Royale National Park.* Duluth, Minnesota: Lake Superior Port Cities, Inc., 1996.

Lockery, Andy. *Marine Archaeology and the Diver.* Toronto, Ontario: Atlantic Publishing, 1985.

Lydecker, Rick. *Pigboat...The Story of the Whalebacks.* Superior, WI: Head of the Lakes Maritime Society, Ltd., 1981 (second edition).

Lytle, William M., and Forrest R. Holdcamper. *Merchant Steam Vessels of the United States, 1790-1868* ("The Lytle-Holdcamper List"). Staten Island, NY: The Steamship Historical Society of America, Inc., 1975.

MacLean, Harrison John. *The Fate of the Griffon.* Chicago, Illinois: The Swallow Press, Inc., 1974.

Mansfield, J. B., ed. *History of the Great Lakes, Volumes I and II.* Chicago, Illinois: J. H. Beers & Co., 1899.

Marshall, James R. *Shipwrecks of Lake Superior.* Duluth, Minnesota: Lake Superior Port Cities, Inc., 1988.

Metcalfe, Willis. *Canvas & Steam on Quinte Waters.* South Bay, Ontario: The South Marysburgh Marine Society, 1979.

Mills, John M. *Canadian Coastal and Inland Steam Vessels, 1809-1930.* Providence, Rhode Island: The Steamship Historical Society of America, Inc., 1979.

Nautical Work Book. Bogota, NJ: Model Shipways, 1961.

Neel, Robert, ed. *Diving in Ohio.* Ohio Council of Skin and Scuba Divers, Inc., 1979.

Nute, Grace Lee. *Lake Superior.* American Lakes Series. Indianapolis & New York: Bobbs-Merrill Company, 1944.

O'Brien, Brendan. *Speedy Justice, The Tragic Last Voyage of His Majesty's Vessel Speedy.* Toronto: University of Toronto Press for The Osgoode Society, 1992.

Oleszewski, Wes. *Ghost Ships, Gales & Forgotten Tales.* Marquette, Michigan: Avery Color Studios, 1995.

_____*Ice Water Museum.* Marquette, Michigan: Avery Color Studios, 1993.

_____*Mysteries and Histories: Shipwrecks of the Great Lakes.* Marquette, Michigan: Avery Color Studios, 1997.

_____*Sounds of Disaster, Great Lakes Shipwrecks.* Marquette, Michigan: Avery Color Studios, 1993.

_____*Stormy Seas, Triumphs and Tragedies of Great Lakes Ships.* Marquette, Michigan: Avery Color Studios, 1991.

Pitz, Herbert. *Lake Michigan Disasters.* Manitowoc, Wisconsin: Manitowoc Maritime Museum, 1925.

Pound, Arthur. *Lake Ontario.* American Lakes Series. Indianapolis & New York: Bobbs-Merrill Company, 1945.

Prothero, Frank and Nancy. *Tales of the North Shore.* Port Stanley, Ontario: Nan-Sea Publications, 1987.

Quaife, Milo M. *Lake Michigan.* American Lakes Series. Indianapolis & New York: Bobbs-Merrill Company, 1944.

Ratigan, William. *Great Lakes Shipwrecks and Survivals.* New York: Galahad Books, 1960.

Rippeth, J. L. *The Lake Michigan Wreck List.* Niles, Illinois: J. L. Rippeth Associates, 1988.

Salen, Rick. *The Tobermory Shipwrecks.* Tobermory, Ontario: The Mariner Chart Shop, 1996 edition.

Sanderson, Herbert J. *Pictorial Marine History.* Sturgeon Bay, Wisconsin: Wisconsin Marine Historical Society, 1984.

Stabelfeldt, Kimm A. *Explore Great Lakes Shipwrecks, Volume I Covering Wrecks on Part of the Lower Lake Michigan.* Wauwatosa, WI: Stabelfeldt & Associates, Inc., 1992 (sixth edition, 1996).

_____*Explore Great Lakes Shipwrecks, Volume II Covering Wrecks the Upper Part of Lake Michigan and Green Bay off the Coasts of Wisconsin and Michigan.* Wauwatosa, WI: Stabelfeldt & Associates, Inc., 1993 (fourth edition, 1996).

Stanton, Samuel Ward. *American Steam Vessels.* New York: Smith & Stanton, 1895.

Stayer, Pat and Jim. *Shipwrecks of Sanilac.* Lexington, Michigan: Out of the Blue Productions, 1995.

Stonehouse, Frederick. *A Short Guide to the Shipwrecks of Thunder Bay.* Alpena, Michigan: B&L Watery World, 1986.

_____*Great Wrecks of the Great Lake.* Marquette, Michigan: Harboridge Press, 1973.

_____*Haunted Lakes, Great Lakes Ghost Stories, Superstitions and Sea Serpents.* Duluth, Minnesota: Lake Superior Port Cities, Inc., 1997.

_____*Isle Royale Shipwrecks.* Au Train, Michigan: Avery Color Studios, 1983.

_____*Keweenaw Shipwrecks.* Au Train, Michigan: Avery Color Studios, 1988.

_____*Lake Superior's Shipwreck Coast.* Au Train, Michigan: Avery Color Studios, 1985.

_____*Marquette Shipwrecks.* Au Train, Michigan: Avery Color Studios, 1974.

_____*Munising Shipwrecks.* Au Train, Michigan: Avery Color Studios, 1983.

_____*Shipwreck of the Mesquite.* Duluth, Minnesota: Lake Superior Port Cities, Inc., 1991.

_____with Daniel R. Fountain. *Dangerous Coast: Pictured Rocks Shipwrecks.* Marquette, Michigan: Avery Color Studios, 1997.

Swayze, David. *Shipwreck.* Traverse City, Michigan: Harbor House, 1992.

Van der Linden, Rev. Peter J., ed., and the Marine Historical Society of Detroit. *Great Lakes Ships We Remember.* Cleveland, Ohio: Freshwater Press, 1979; revised 1984.

_____*Great Lakes Ships We Remember II.* Cleveland, Ohio: Freshwater Press, 1984.

_____*Great Lakes Ships We Remember III.* Cleveland, Ohio: Freshwater Press, 1994.

Wachter, Georgann & Michael. *Erie Wrecks, A Divers Guide.* Avon Lake, Ohio: Corporate*Impact*, 1997.

Wolff, Julius F., Jr. *Lake Superior Shipwrecks.* Duluth, Minnesota: Lake Superior Port Cities, Inc., 1990.

Wrigley, Ronald. *Shipwrecked, Vessels That Met Tragedy on Northern Lake Superior.* Cobalt, Ontario: Highway Book Shop, 1985.

Young, Anna G. *Great Lakes Saga.* Owen Sound, Ontario: Richardson, Bond & Wright, Ltd., 1965.

_____*Off Watch.* Toronto: The Ryerson Press, 1957.

PERIODICALS

Aelick, B., and B. Lyons. "The *Sagamore.*" *Save Ontario Shipwrecks Newsletter.* (Summer, 1994), pp. 21-22.

Alford, Terry. "Kingston's Newest Wreck Dive (the *Wolfe Islander II*)." *Diver Magazine.* Vol. 12, No. 1 (March, 1986), pp. 18-21.

_____"Time Capsule in Kingston, Queen of Kingston's Wrecks *(Wolfe Islander II)."* *Diver Magazine.* Vol. 14, No. 1 (March, 1988), pp. 19-20.

Ashlee, Laura Rose. *"Three Brothers,* A Lady and A Crayfish." *Michigan History Magazine.* (November-December, 1996), pp. 26-27.

Barker, Gerry. "The Loss of the Steamer *Atlantic.*" *Inland Seas.* Vol. 20, No. 3 (Fall, 1964), pp. 211-214.

Barry, James P. "Great Lakes Time Line, Lake Erie." *Inland Seas,* Vol. 41, No. 4 (Winter, 1985), pp. 291-295.

_____"Great Lakes Time Line, Lake Huron." *Inland Seas,* Vol. 41, No. 4 (Winter, 1985), pp. 282-285.

Bennett, George, with Skip Gilham. "Depression Era Great Lakes Sailor." *Mariners Weather Log* (Winter, 1993), pp. 28-29.

Boyd, Ellsworth. "The *Regina.*" *Skin Diver* Magazine. Vol. 37, No. 10 (October, 1988), pp. 78, 150-152.

Coplin, Larry, and Bruce McLaughlan. "A Shipwreck Shrouded in Mystery *(Kamloops)." Diver Magazine.* Vol. 10, No. 9 (December, 1984), pp. 15-19.

Dow, C.J. "The *Dean Richmond.*" *Inland Seas.* Vol. 7, No. 1 (Spring, 1951), pp. 35, 41-45.

Drew, Richard C. "Chicago's Most Popular Dive (the *Material Service).*" *Skin Diver* Magazine, Vol. 39, No. 1 (January, 1990), pp. 12, 146-150.

Duncan, F. "A Lake Erie Disaster (the *Courtland-Morning Star* Collision)." *Sea Breezes.* (May, 1963), pp. 382-387.

Emering, Ed. "The Fated Lady (the *Wisconsin)." Scuba Times* Magazine. Vol. 14, No. 3 (May-June, 1993), pp. 48-49.

Fanslow, Pauline G., and Nancy A. Schneider. "Great Lakes Time Line, Lake Michigan." *Inland Seas,* Vol. 41, No. 4 (Winter, 1985), pp. 285-291.

Feltner, Charles. *"Eber Ward." Diver Magazine.* Vol. 7, No. 6 (September, 1981), pp. 18-22. Reprinted from the November/December, 1980 issue of *Diving Times* of Royal Oak, Michigan.

_____"Raise the *Cayuga." Diving Times* (April/May, 1981).

_____"The *Cedarville* Tragedy." *Diving Times* (June/July, 1981).

_____"The Strange Tale of Two Ships *(Maitland* and *Northwest)." Diving Times* (February/March, 1981).

_____"The Wreck of the *Col. Ellsworth." Diving Times* (June-July, 1980).

_____"The Wreck of the Brig *Sandusky." Diving Times* (October/November, 1981).

_____"The Wreck of the *William H. Barnum." Diving Times* (Aug./Sept., 1980).

Folkes, Patrick. "Hope Island Wreck Identified." *Save Ontario Shipwrecks Newsletter* (Spring/Summer, 1985), p. 14. Reprinted from the *Newsletter of the Association for Great Lakes Maritime History.*

_____"The Schooner *Sweepstakes,* A Mystery Solved." *Save Ontario Shipwrecks Newsletter.* (Spring-Summer, 1984), pp. 12-13.

Garn, Myk. "Return to the *Emperor,* The Pride of Canada." *Skin Diver* Magazine. Vol. 35, No. 4 (April, 1986), p. 30.

Gerred, Janice H. "The *Myron* Meets November 1919." *Inland Seas,* Vol. 41, No. 1 (Spring, 1985), pp. 9-10.

Gilchrist, David. "Lake Erie Wreck Dive (the *Carlingford)." Diver Magazine.* Vol. 20, No. 1 (March, 1994), pp. 22-23.

Golding, Peter. "The *Price* Adventure." *Diver Magazine.* Vol. 4, No. 8 (November-December, 1978), pp. 34-38.

_____"Inner Space Adventure, *Comet* in Lake Ontario." *Diver Magazine.* Vol. 5, No. 4 (June, 1979), pp. 21-24.

_____"*Maple Dawn* (sic)." *Diver Magazine.* Vol. 6, No. 4 (April-May, 1980), pp. 36-37.

_____"The Wreck of the *George A. Marsh." Diver Magazine.* Vol. 5, No. 8 (November-December, 1979), pp. 38-40.

Hall, Judy. "Save the *Sweepstakes,* Completion of Phase 1." *The Canadian Diving News* (January, 1972), pp. 9-11.

Halsey, John R., and Scott M. Peters. "Resurrection of a Great Lakes Steamer (the *Three Brothers)." Michigan History Magazine.* (November-December, 1996), pp. 22-25.

Harneck, Robin. "A Virgin Experience (the *Regina). " Skin Diver* Magazine. Vol. 37, No. 7 (July, 1988), pp. 70, 77.

Harvey, Robert. "Survey Report---S. O. S. Quinte, *Annie Falconer." Save Ontario Shipwrecks Newsletter* (Spring/Summer, 1985), pp. 11-14.

Holden, Thom. "A Maiden Voyage into History (the *George M. Cox). " Telescope.* (January-February, 1984), pp. 3-10.

_____"Reef of the Three C's: Part III, Sinking of the *George M. Cox." The Nor'Easter.* Vol. 8, No. 3 (May-June, 1983), pp. 1-5.

Jackson, Rick. "Toronto Has a Change of Heart." *Save Ontario Shipwrecks Newsletter* (Fall, 1986), pp. 8-9.

Johnson, Dave. "The Final Hours of the *Mesquite." The Nor'Easter.* Vol. 15, No. 1 (January-February, 1990), pp. 1-5.

Johnson, Ken. "Graveyard of Lake Superior, Whitefish Point and Whitefish Bay." *Diver Magazine.* Vol. 11, No. 1 (January-February, 1985), pp. 16-19.

_____"Strange Story of the Steamer *Myron." Diver Magazine.* Vol. 10, No. 6 (September, 1984), pp. 20-21.

_____"The Controversial Loss of the Motorship *Material Service." Diver Magazine.* Vol. 11, No. 8 (December, 1985), pp. 16-19.

Keller, James. "Shipwrecked! (The *Sevona*)" *Wisconsin Trails Magazine.* (September-October, 1984), pp. 18-22, 65.

Kemp, Bruce. "Lake Huron Mystery (the *Charles S. Price*)" *Diver Magazine.* Vol. 8, No. 2 (March, 1981), pp. 17-20.

King, Ted. "The Mystery of the *Dean Richmond.*" *Great Lakes, Inland Waterways and Seaway Journal.* (November, 1961), pp. 10-11, 13.

Kohl, Cris. "A Lake Huron Gem: The *Emma E. Thompson.*" *Diver Magazine.* Vol. 23, No. 4 (June, 1997), pp. 18-19.

_____"*America,* the Beautiful --- Shipwreck." *Diver Magazine.* Vol. 23, No. 8 (December, 1997), pp. 25-28.

_____"Backwoods Secret (the wreck *Columbus*)." *Diver Magazine.* Vol. 17, No. 5 (August, 1991), pp. 33-35.

_____"Battle for the *Atlantic.*" *Diver Magazine.* Vol. 19 , No. 3 (May, 1993), pp. 36-37.

_____"Ghost Fleet of the St. Clair River." *Diver Magazine,* Vol. 22, No. 3, pp. 24-25.

_____"Honeymoon Wreck: Lake Huron's *Joyland.*" *Diver Magazine.* Vol. 22, No. 2 (April, 1996), pp. 30-31.

_____"Kingston's Newest Shipwreck: the Tug, *Frontenac.*" *Diver Magazine.* Vol. 23, No. 3 (May, 1997), pp. 18-19.

_____"Lake Erie's Lost Steamer, *Colonial.*" *Diver Magazine,* Vol. 20, No. 4 (June, 1994), pp. 22-23.

_____"Lake Ontario's Lost Team: *Condor* and *Atlasco.*" *Diver Magazine,* Vol. 22, No. 7 (November, 1996), pp. 24-25.

_____"*Manola*--Half a Shipwreck." *Diver Magazine.* Vol. 21, No. 9 (February, 1996), p. 28.

_____"Rammed: The *Lac La Belle's* St. Clair River Episode." *Inland Seas.* Vol. 43, No. 4 (Winter, 1987), pp. 247-251.

_____"Shipwrecks Threatened by Freshwater Barnacles." *Diving Times.* Vol. 12, No. 2 (Summer, 1989).

_____"The Broken Lady of Driftwood Cove, the *Caroline Rose.*" *Diver Magazine,* Vol. 24, No. 2 (April, 1998), pp. 26-27.

_____"The Dredge, *Munson.*" *Diver Magazine.* Vol. 23, No. 6 (September, 1997), pp. 26-27.

_____"The *George A. Marsh* Mystery." *Diver Magazine.* Vol. 24, No. 5 (July-August, 1998).

_____"The Steamer, *Northern Indiana,* Lake Erie Tragedy." *Diver Magazine,* Vol. 22, No. 9 (February, 1997), pp. 20-22.

_____"The Steamer, *Philip Minch.*" *Diver Magazine,* Vol. 23, No. 9 (February, 1998), pp. 24, 26.

_____"Tobermory's Forgotten Shipwrecks." *Diver Magazine*, Vol. 22, No. 4 (June, 1996), pp. 24-26.

_____"Tragic Wreck on Lake Erie (the *Merida*)." *Diver Magazine*. Vol. 24, No. 3 (May, 1998), pp. 26-27.

_____"Three Strikes Against the *Burlington*." *Diver Magazine*, Vol. 21, No. 8 (Dec., 1995), p. 26

_____"Whitefish Point." *Diver Magazine*. Vol. 23, No. 1 (March, 1997), pp. 18-19, 26.

_____and Sharon Hamilton. *"City of Genoa." Diving Times.* Vol 10, No. 4 (Winter, 1987-88), p. 14.

Kozmik, Jim. *"Arabia,* Fathom Five's Deep Lady." *Diver Magazine*, Vol. 7, No. 2 (March, 1981), pp. 28-29.

Kuss, Dan. "Wreck of the *Rappahannock*." *Diver Magazine*. Vol. 16, No. 8 (December, 1990), pp. 19-21.

_____"Lake Superior's Storm to Remember." *Diver Magazine*. Vol. 10, No. 7 (October-November, 1984), pp. 12-14.

Labadie, C. Patrick. "Lake Superior's *Bermuda."* *Skin Diver* Magazine. Vol. 39, No. 10 (October, 1990), pp. 12-13, 154-155.

_____"The Iron *Wisconsin."* *Telescope.* (October, 1964), pp. 235-241.

Larson, Phil, and Paul Schmitt. *"Regina* Yields Her Secrets." *Great Lakes Travel & Living* Magazine. Vol. III, No. 8 (November-December, 1988), pp. 18-23.

Marshall, James R. "Isle Royale's Most Unusual Tragedy, The *George M. Cox." Lake Superior* Magazine. (March-April, 1988), pp. 62-64.

_____"Farewell *Mesquite."* *Lake Superior Magazine.* (December-January, 1991), pp. 24-28.

McBrady, ENS Michael T. (USCGC *Bramble*). *"Bramble* Marks Historical Site Under Michigan Waters [the tug, *Sport]."* *Shipmates* (U.S. Coast Guard publication. (November 1992), p. 6

McDaniel, Neil. "Fathom Five's Deep Treasure, the Barque *Arabia." Diver Magazine.* Vol. 13, No. 3 (May, 1987), pp. 22-23.

McLaughlin, Bruce. "Lake Huron's Five-Mile-Long Shipwreck *(Daniel J. Morrell)." Diver Magazine.* Vol. 10, No. 4 (June, 1984), pp. 32-34.

McManamon, John, S.J. "Sinking of the *Wells Burt." Inland Seas.* Vol. 46, No. 3 (Fall, 1990), pp. 174-183.

Messmer, Jack. "The Wreck of the *Passaic." Telescope.* (September-October, 1978), pp. 125-126.

Miller, Al. "The Search for *Barge 115." The Nor'Easter.* Vol. 19, No. 1 (January-February, 1994), pp. 1-5.

_____"The 'Lucky' Boat (the *City of Cleveland*)." *The Nor'Easter*. Vol. 13, No. 6 (November-December, 1988), pp. 1-4.

Mullings, Ken. "The Fate of the *Falconer*." *Diver Magazine*. Vol. 18, No. 6 (September, 1992), pp. 18-19.

_____"Quinte's Favourite Dive Site." *Save Ontario Shipwrecks Newsletter*. (Spring/Summer, 1988), pp. 20-22.

Orr, Dan. "The Barque *Arabia*: 1853-1884." *Diver Magazine*. Vol. 11, No. 6 (September, 1985), pp. 30-32.

Palmer, Richard. "Great Lakes Time Line, Lake Ontario." *Inland Seas*, Vol. 41, No. 4 (Winter, 1985), pp. 295-299.

Remick, Teddy. "Wreck of the S. S. *Wisconsin*." *Skin Diver* Magazine. Vol. 14, No. 9 (September, 1965), pp. 55, 66.

Schmitt, Paul J. "Lake Huron's *Sport*." *Skin Diver* Magazine. Vol. 38, No. 10 (October, 1989), pp. 16, 58.

Soegtrop, Michael. "*Mapledawn*, Wreck in Southern Georgian Bay." *Diver Magazine*. Vol. 18, No. 4 (June, 1992), pp. 20-21.

_____"Tobermory's Classic Shipwreck, *City of Cleveland*." *Diver Magazine*. Vol. 13, No. 1 (March, 1987), pp. 24-29.

_____"Twice Lost by Fire (the *Atlantic*)." *Diver Magazine*. Vol. 7, No. 3 (April-May, 1981), pp. 27-29.

Steinborn, Bill. "Lake Michigan's *Milwaukee*." *Skin Diver* Magazine. Vol. 40, No. 5 (May, 1991), pp. 30, 66.

_____"Lake Michigan's *Norland* (sic)." *Skin Diver* Magazine. Vol. 39, No. 3 (March, 1990), pp. 8, 56-57.

_____"Lake Superior's *Smith Moore*." *Skin Diver* Magazine. Vol. 40, No. 7 (July, 1991), pp. 188-190.

_____"Milwaukee's *Prins Willem V*" *Skin Diver* Magazine. Vol. 39, No. 7 (July, 1990), pp. 16, 18-19.

_____"Wisconsin's S. S. *Wisconsin*." *Skin Diver* Magazine. Vol. 40, No. 4 (April, 1991), pp. 24, 182-183.

Stephan, Robert. "Wreck of the *Admiral*." *Soundings*, Wisconsin Marine Historical Society. Vol. 21, No. 3, 1981, pp. 1,3.

Swierczewski, John. "Isle Royale, Lake Superior's Shipwreck Mecca." *Diver Magazine*. Vol. 10, No. 2 (March, 1984), pp. 34-35.

Tomasi, Bettey. "Sinking of the *Wisconsin*." *Diver Magazine*. Vol. 7, No. 8 (December, 1981), pp. 26-27, 38-39.

Triebe, Richard. "*Milwaukee* Car Ferry." *Skin Diver* Magazine. Vol. 36, No. 1 (January, 1987), pp. 110, 113-114, 120.

_____"S. S. *Wisconsin*." *Skin Diver* Magazine. Vol. 36, No. 5 (May, 1987), pp. 142-147.

_____"The Burning of the *Niagara*, Gold & Goodies Sizzle & Sink." *Skin Diver Magazine.* Vol. 37, No. 5 (May, 1988), pp. 184-188.

Trotter, David. "The Discovery of the *John McGean." Diver Magazine.* Vol. 13, No. 6 (September, 1987), pp. 30-33.

Weir, Stephen. "The Mysterious Sinking of the *Charles S. Price." Inland Seas.* Vol. 42, No. 2 (Summer, 1986), pp. 102-114.

Wolff, Dr. Julius F., Jr. "Great Lakes Time Line, Lake Superior." *Inland Seas,* Vol. 41, No. 4 (Winter, 1985), pp. 274-282.

NEWSLETTERS, JOURNALS, REPORTS, & DIRECTORIES

Anchor News. The Newsletter of the Manitowoc Maritime Museum, Manitowoc, Wisconsin.

Beeson's Marine Directory of the Northwestern Lakes. Chicago: Harvey C. Beeson. Published annually 1882-1921, including a list of vessels lost each year.

Diving Times. The Journal of Great Lakes Sport Diving, Detroit, Michigan, 1978-1990.

Flipper, The. The Newsletter of the Great Lakes Aquanauts of Greater Detroit.

Hundley, Paul F. "The Griffon Cove Wreck: A case study in archaeological reconstruction of timber hull remains." Australian Institute for Maritime Archaeology. Special Publication No. 2, 1984.

Lake Huron Lore. Newsletter of the Lake Huron Lore Society, Port Huron, Michigan.

Inland Seas. The Journal of the Great Lakes Historical Society, Vermilion, Ohio.

Marine Review. Cleveland: Penton Publishing Co., 1890-1935. A weekly publication from March 6, 1890 until March 25, 1909; monthly from April, 1909 until October, 1935.

Mullings, Ken. "Monitoring the *Falconer*, An Archaeological Site Update of the Fore-and-Aft Schooner, *Annie Falconer*." Kingston, Ontario: Preserve Our Wrecks, 1992, plus 1993, 1994, and 1995 updates.

Nor'Easter, The. Journal of the Lake Superior Marine Museum Association. C. Patrick Labadie, Contributing Editor.

Olson, Valerie, ed. *The Goshawk Project, A Reconnaissance Survey of the Great Lake's Oldest Schooner.* February, 1995.

S. S. Regina, 1987 Report to the State of Michigan. Marysville, Michigan: Commercial Diving and Marine Services, 1987.

Scanner, The. Monthly News Bulletin of the Toronto Marine Historical Society.

Soundings. Newsletter of the Wisconsin Maritime Historical Society.

Telescope. Journal of the Great Lakes Maritime Institute, Dossin Marine Museum, Belle Isle, Detroit, Michigan.

Thompson, Douglas G. *The Annie Falconer, Archaeological Survey & Salvage Project, 1982.* Preserve Our Wrecks Kingston (Ontario) Ltd., Jan. 31, 1983.

COLLECTIONS AND PUBLIC DOCUMENTS

Ackerman, Paul. Chicago, Illinois: Midwest Explorers League. "Lake Erie Dive Chart" (1998 ed.), "Lake Huron Dive Chart" (1990 ed.), "Lake Michigan Dive Chart" (1988 ed.), "Lake Michigan Shipwrecks, South Shores" (1988 ed.), "Lake Ontario Dive Chart" (1990 ed.), "Lake Superior Dive Chart" (1990 ed.).

Diving Michigan's Underwater Preserves 1997. (Booklet) Lexington, Michigan: Out of the Blue Productions, for the Michigan Underwater Preserve Council, Inc., 1997.

Great Lakes Historical Society, Vermilion, Ohio.

Institute for Great Lakes Research, Bowling Green State University, Bowling Green, Ohio, (former name; incorporated since 1996 into the Center for Archival Collections, Bowling Green State University, Bowling Green, Ohio).

Cris Kohl Collection: Great Lakes Shipwrecks and Maritime History.

Marine Historical Collection of the Milwaukee Public Library, Milwaukee, Wisconsin (in particular the Runge Collection, "Herman G. Runge Great Lakes Vessel Files").

Wisconsin Marine Historical Society, Milwaukee, Wisconsin.

NEWSPAPERS

Chicago *Inter Ocean*

Cleveland *Plain Dealer*

Daily News (Kingston, ON)

Daily Times-Journal (Fort William, ON)

Detroit *Free Press*

Detroit *News-Tribune*

Door County Advocate (Wisconsin)

Duluth *Evening Herald*

Duluth *News-Tribune*

Hallowel Free Press (Picton, ON)

Intelligencer (Belleville, ON)

Kenosha *Life*

Kingston *Whig*

Manitoulin (Island) *Expositor*

Milwaukee *Journal*

Milwaukee *Sentinel*

Mining Journal (Marquette, MI)

News Herald and Press (Tawas City, MI)

Oswego *Palladium*

Rochester (NY) *Times-Union*

Toledo *Blade*

Toronto *Evening Telegram*

UNPUBLISHED MATERIAL

Correspondence with Ellsworth Boyd, 1986-1997.

Steve Carrigan of Aurora, Illinois, interviewed on February 19, 1998.

Dale Currier of Oswego, New York, interviewed on February 17, 1998.

Darryl Ertel and Matt Turchi of Flint, Michigan, interviewed in March, 1998.

Chuck and Jeri Feltner of Dearborn and Drummond I., MI, interviewed in Aug., 1995.

Captain Jim Herbert of Barcelona, New York, interviewed on February 15, 1998.

Tim Juhl of Carsonville, Michigan, interviewed in July, 1995.

Barb Marshall of Stevensville, Ontario, interviewed in October, 1997.

Valerie Olson-van Heest of Holland, Michigan, interviewed in October, 1997.

Doug Pettingill of Picton, Ontario, interviewed in July, 1995.

Captain Roy Pickering of Blenheim Ontario, interviewed in April, 1998.

Steve Radovan of Sheboygan, WI, interviewed in July, 1997, and April 18, 1998.

Tom Rasbeck of Oswego, New York, interviewed on February 18, 1998.

Captain Jim and Pat Stayer of Lexington, MI, interviewed in July, 1995, and February, 1998.

John Steele interviewed at DeTour, MI, on July 6, 1995, and at Grand Marais, MI, on July 13-14, 1997.

David Trotter of Canton, Michigan, interviewed in July, 1995 and February, 1998.

Frank Troxell of Davisburg, Michigan, interviewed in February and May, 1998.

Sharon Troxell, of White Lake Twp., Michigan, interviewed in February, 1998.

Georgann Wachter of Avon Lake, Ohio, interviewed in October, 1997

George West of Sheboygan, WI, interviewed on July 13-14, 1997, and Apr. 18, 1998

MISCELLANEOUS

Beaudry, Marc. *Diving the Great Lakes --- A Video Sampling* (videotape). Covers the wrecks of the *City of Sheboygan, Dunderburg, Munson, North Wind*, and *St. Peter*. 30.5 minutes. March, 1997.

Ertel, Darryl, and Matt Turchi. *The Gunilda Project* (videotape). A Turchi/Ertel Production, 1997.

Ertel, Darryl, and Matt Turchi. *A Cold, Dark Hart* (videotape). A Turchi/Ertel Production, 1997.

Fletcher, Michael. *Steamer Atlantic Preservation Project* (videotape). 1993.

Guyer, Jerry. *Jerry's Shipwreck Charts. Lake Michigan Shipwrecks From North of Port Washington to the Illinois State Line.* April 19, 1996, 5th ed.

Out of the Blue Productions. Videotapes: "S.S. *Daniel J. Morrell* Remembered" (1996), "Dangerous Waters: Shipwrecks of Point Traverse (1997), "*Pewabic,* The Death Ship of Lake Huron" (1997), and "*Canisteo*" (1997). 4658 S. Lakeshore, Lexington, MI 48450. Telephone: (313)359-8660.

INDEX

TO VOLUME II

SHIPS' NAMES ARE IN *italics.*
AN ASTERISK [*] DENOTES A PHOTOGRAPH.

IMPORTANT CONTACTS

for the Lake Michigan and Lake Superior

Hyperbaric Chambers:

D.A.N. (Divers Alert Network): (919) 684-8111 or (919) 684-2948

Bronson Methodist Hospital, KALAMAZOO, Michigan: (616) 341-7654

Hennepin County Hospital, MINNEAPOLIS, Minnesota: (612) 347-3131

Marquette General Hospital, MARQUETTE, Michigan: (906) 225-3560 or (616) 341-7778

St. Luke's Hospital, MILWAUKEE, Wisconsin: (414) 649-6577

Parks and Preserves:

Michigan Underwater Preserve Council, Inc., 560 N. State Street, ST. IGNACE, MI 49781

Alger Underwater Preserve, P.O. Box 272, MUNISING, MI 49868

Keweenaw Underwater Preserve, c/o Keweenaw Tourism Council, P.O. Box 336, HOUGHTON, MI 49931

Manitou Underwater Preserve, c/o Sleeping Bear Dunes National Lakeshore, P.O. Box 277, EMPIRE, MI 49630

South West Michigan Underwater Preserve, c/o Michigan Sea Grant, 333 Clinton, GRAND HAVEN, MI 49417

Straits Underwater Preserve, c/o St. Ignace Chamber of Commerce, 560 N. State St., ST. IGNACE, MI 49871

Whitefish Underwater Preserve, c/o Paradise Area Chamber of Commerce, P.O. Box 82, PARADISE, MI 49768

General:

Cris Kohl can be contacted through his publisher,
Seawolf Communications, Inc., P.O. Box 66, West Chicago, IL 60186,
telephone (630) 293-8996, fax: (630) 293-8837, e-mail: SeawolfRex@aol.com
or Cris Kohl's e-mail: criskohl@aol.com

ABOUT THE AUTHOR

PHOTO BY JIM STAYER.

Cris Kohl first became intrigued by shipwrecks and the stories behind them after his initial exposure to the underwater world in Bermuda and the Florida Keys in 1974. Hailing from Windsor, Ontario, Canada, his three university degrees include a Master's degree in History, specializing in Great Lakes maritime history. He published his first Great Lakes shipwrecks book in 1985. He has written seven books and, since 1982, hundreds of articles about Great Lakes shipwrecks and scuba diving in a variety of magazines, journals, and newsletters. The scuba club newsletter he produced in 1984 won the first place award for all of Ontario. He is a certified Divemaster, Master Diver, Nitrox, and Full Cave Diver.

In addition to a career in education, Cris Kohl has worked as a hospital operating room porter, a laborer in a steel plant, an automotive assembly line worker, a forest fire fighter along the Alaska Highway in British Columbia, a taxi-driver, a waiter, a bartender, a grape harvester, a pianist, and a real estate agent. He hitch-hiked across Canada four times, as well as up and down the Alaska Highway and across Europe from Sweden to Spain. He drove an old station wagon across Australia's outback, and explored shipwrecks in three oceans (the Atlantic, the Pacific, and the Indian).

Cris Kohl's intense research, award-winning photography, enthusiasm, vigor, and sense of drama have made him a popular speaker at local historical societies, scuba club meetings, and major scuba shows. A firm supporter of diver access to shipwrecks and shipwreck information, he is also a staunch marine conservationist, fully aware that the shipwrecks in our Great Lakes waters are the best preserved shipwrecks in the world!

MORE GREAT LAKES SHIPWRECKS BOOKS

Shipwreck books by Cris Kohl are available at bookstores and scuba dive shops, or they may be ordered through the mail. The following titles are available at press time:

DIVE ONTARIO! THE GUIDE TO SHIPWRECKS & SCUBA IN ONT. $29.95 U.S.
DIVE ONTARIO TWO! MORE ONTARIO SHIPWRECK STORIES.... $24.95 U.S.
TREACHEROUS WATERS: KINGSTON'S SHIPWRECKS............. $17.95 U.S.
THE 100 BEST GREAT LAKES SHIPWRECKS, VOL. I (EAST)..... $21.95 U.S.
THE 100 BEST GREAT LAKES SHIPWRECKS, VOL. II (WEST) ... $21.95 U.S.

Add postage and handling: $2.00 for 1st book, and $1.00 for each additional book.

Illinois orders please add 6.75% sales tax.

Mail check or money order, made out to Seawolf Communications, Inc., to:
Seawolf Communications, Inc., P.O. Box 66, West Chicago, IL 60186.

MORE GREAT BOOKS
ON GREAT LAKES SHIPWRECKS!
ORDER FORM

Books by Cris Kohl Available:

DIVE ONTARIO! THE GUIDE TO SHIPWRECKS & SCUBA IN ONT. $29.95 U.S.
   (hardcover, 408 pages, about 200 shipwrecks, 248 b&w photos, many maps & drawings)

DIVE ONTARIO TWO! MORE ONTARIO SHIPWRECK STORIES .... $24.95 U.S.
   (hardcover, 312 pages, over 130 shipwrecks, 230 b&w photos, many maps & drawings)

TREACHEROUS WATERS: KINGSTON'S SHIPWRECKS............. $17.95 U.S.
   (softcover, 248 pages, maps, about 200 shipwrecks, over b&w 100 photos, many drawings)

THE 100 BEST GREAT LAKES SHIPWRECKS, VOL. I.............. $21.95 U.S.
(Lakes Ontario, Erie, and Huron, softcover, 284 pages, 75 color photos, 49 b&w, maps, drawings)

THE 100 BEST GREAT LAKES SHIPWRECKS, VOL. II............. $21.95 U.S.
(Lakes Michigan and Superior, softcover, 284 pages, 75 color photos, 57 b&w, maps, drawings)

Please send the following books:

_____

_____

_____

I understand that I may return any books for a full refund---for any reason, no questions asked---if returned undamaged within 30 days. Please indicate if you would like any of the books signed and inscribed. Personalized books cannot be returned.

Name:_____

Address:_____

City:_____ State/Prov:_____

Zip/Postal Code:_____

Illinois orders please add 6.75% state tax.
Shipping: Please add $2.00 for the first book, and $1.00 for each additional book.
Mail order form with check or money order made out to Seawolf Communications to:
Seawolf Communications, Inc., P.O. Box 66, West Chicago, IL 60186
Tel: (630) 293-8996 Fax: (630) 293-8837 E-mail: SeawolfRex@aol.com

MORE GREAT BOOKS
ON GREAT LAKES SHIPWRECKS!
ORDER FORM

Books by Cris Kohl Available:

DIVE ONTARIO! THE GUIDE TO SHIPWRECKS & SCUBA IN ONT. $29.95 U.S.
(hardcover, 408 pages, about 200 shipwrecks, 248 b&w photos, many maps & drawings)

DIVE ONTARIO TWO! MORE ONTARIO SHIPWRECK STORIES ....$24.95 U.S.
(hardcover, 312 pages, over 130 shipwrecks, 230 b&w photos, many maps & drawings)

TREACHEROUS WATERS: KINGSTON'S SHIPWRECKS.............$17.95 U.S.
(softcover, 248 pages, maps, about 200 shipwrecks, over b&w 100 photos, many drawings)

THE 100 BEST GREAT LAKES SHIPWRECKS, VOL. I..............$21.95 U.S.
(Lakes Ontario, Erie, and Huron, softcover, 284 pages, 75 color photos, 49 b&w, maps, drawings)

THE 100 BEST GREAT LAKES SHIPWRECKS, VOL. II.............$21.95 U.S.
(Lakes Michigan and Superior, softcover, 284 pages, 75 color photos, 57 b&w, maps, drawings)

Please send the following books:

_____

_____

_____

I understand that I may return any books for a full refund---for any reason, no questions asked---if returned undamaged within 30 days. Please indicate if you would like any of the books signed and inscribed. Personalized books cannot be returned.

Name:_____

Address:_____

City:_____ State/Prov:_____

Zip/Postal Code:_____

Illinois orders please add 6.75% state tax.
Shipping: Please add $2.00 for the first book, and $1.00 for each additional book.
Mail order form with check or money order made out to Seawolf Communications to:
Seawolf Communications, Inc., P.O. Box 66, West Chicago, IL 60186
Tel: (630) 293-8996 Fax: (630) 293-8837 E-mail: SeawolfRex@aol.com